Hermann Spindler

The Demeter Cookbook

Recipes based on biodynamic ingredients
from the kitchen of
the LUKAS KLINIK

TEMPLE LODGE

Temple Lodge Publishing
Hillside House, The Square
Forest Row, East Sussex RH18 5ES

www.templelodge.com

First English edition 2008

Originally published in German under the title *Das Kochbuch* by Lukas Klinik, Arlesheim, in 2007

Translated from German by Matthew Barton

ISBN 978 1 902636 96 2

All photos by Jürg Buess

Interior design and typesetting by Christoph Jäggy

Cover layout by Andrew Morgan

Printed and bound by 1010 Printing International Ltd., China

Acknowledgements

I would especially like to thank my colleagues Luis De Jesus and Harold Appuhamy who gave me unstinting support in developing the recipes.

Hermann Spindler, head cook

Foreword

The Lukas Klinik in Arlesheim is known far beyond the borders of Switzerland not just for its excellent holistic nursing based on the principles of anthroposophic medicine, but also – among those in the know – for its outstanding vegetarian cooking. This reputation is fully justified.

Thirty years ago, after passing my state medical exam at Bern University, I attended the anthroposophic doctors' seminar at the Lukas Klinik. We doctors-in-training ate with patients and co-workers there, and already at that time I was struck by the special quality of the food at the clinic, and also by the caring atmosphere in which it was served. This remains true today. My further medical training took me to other hospitals, and my scientific career led me to Bern's university hospital, but I can truly say that I never ate such good food and above all of such constant and reliable quality as I did at the Lukas Klinik in Arlesheim.

The menu accords with modern nutritional ideas. A vegetarian, lacto-vegetarian wholefood diet was already being offered here at a time when some people in the field of conventional medicine dismissed such ideas. Today the Swiss Cancer League gives very similar dietary advice.

Alongside food preparation methods that conserve nutritional value, a wide diversity of recipes, imaginative presentation of dishes and freshly prepared meals, the special nature of Lukas Klinik cuisine is the complete absence of ready-made sauces, genetically engineered produce and so on. By contrast, great emphasis is placed on the careful selection of Demeter-quality foods produced by organic and biodynamic agricultural methods. In addition such produce comes from farms and reliable suppliers personally known to the head cook. The Lukas Klinik kitchen is certified organic.

In holistic disease prevention and anthroposophic medical treatment, general measures such as nutrition form a conscious part of promoting health, alongside medicines. This is particularly relevant for cancer. A study by the Swiss National Fund for scientific research has found that all aspects of cancer patients' quality of life is enormously enhanced by in-patient treatment offered at the Lukas Klinik, Arlesheim. This includes improvement in disease-associated symptoms such as pain, tiredness, etc., but also symptoms involving the digestive system – e.g. a significant increase in appetite and so on. It is clear that these results are due not only to doctors, nurses and therapists but also the outstanding cuisine at the Lukas Klinik, and its concern with the dietary needs of each individual patient.

The many editions of the old cookbook were in great demand and are now consequently out of print, and I am pleased that our head cook Hermann Spindler has now published his old favourites, and newer recipes, making them available to a broader public. I wish readers much enjoyment in their cooking, and their guests a good appetite! And if you would like to experience Herr Spindler's cooking here at first hand, feel free to attend a 'recipe evening', one of his cookery demonstrations, or just make an appointment to eat lunch with us!

Dr. med. Peter Heusser,
Director of the Lukas Klinik, Arlesheim

The Value of Demeter Produce

At the Lukas Klinik most produce used is biodynamic or Demeter food. The head cook Hermann Spindler buys this largely from farmers and cultivators in the surrounding region whom he knows personally. The range of produce varies seasonally and the menu alters accordingly. This highlights two important ideals of anthroposophic nutrition: wherever possible to use seasonal produce, and to obtain it directly through known suppliers and thus nurture real human relationships.

Not all food is suitable for all people. Thus Hermann Spindler seeks produce which he considers to be right for people at the Lukas Klinik. In doing so he is aided by perspectives such as that root vegetables address the nerve-sense system, leaf vegetables the rhythmic system, and blossoms and fruits the metabolism. He prepares the produce with an inner conviction that accords with this outlook. Eating together, perhaps with a grace beforehand, is yet another aspect of an all-embracing nutritional approach. None of this is dogmatic though, but often arises naturally from a close preoccupation with the practical realities of food preparation.

We transform the food we eat and its forces – the senses absorb substances too, but here we are concerned with food digestion – into the body's own substances and forces. Depending on the nature of our food, we need to bring either more or less energy to bear on it. Generally, meat is closer to us than vegetable matter, and shoots and watery produce require less energy from us than denser, more compact substances. But that is the very point in nutrition. Our self or 'I' develops more strongly the more it needs to overcome and transform what it absorbs, rather than being 'lazy'. Nutrition is similar in this way to physical exercise: initially this costs us some effort, but then it does us more good.

Biodynamic agriculture aims to cultivate plants and animals in a way that is as closely as possible adapted to their intrinsic nature, so that when we eat them they 'confront' us and engage our digestive effort, thus strengthening our own forces.

A similar principle applies to the life of plants themselves. As they engage with the soil they develop their distinctive qualities. Thus the biodynamic approach does not countenance soil-free cultivation, e.g. on rockwool. Furthermore, special attention is given to caring for the soil, soil structure and soil improvement. Plants partly draw from the soil the salts they need, which they absorb with water, by actively secreting acids. To do so they need the soil to partner and oppose them in the right way, so that the roots can actively connect. Thus the 'mother' soil is the starting point for healthy plant growth. But the plant also needs the strength which it brings with it from the seed. Since developments in conventional agriculture tend to encourage uniform species and varieties and, for economic reasons, attempts are afoot to patent and privatize our commonly owned seed heritage, hybrid cultivation has become standard practice. Here inbred lines are cross-fertilized to produce subsequent generations that are no longer fertile.* Thus farmers and cultivators can no longer raise their own seed. At the same time plants are losing their vitality. To counteract these developments, biodynamic farmers and their supporters are making great efforts to raise biodynamic seed stock. These seed varieties are being bred for taste and vital forces. Increasingly it is proving possible to secure and safeguard an ever wider range of species for biodynamic farming and gardening.

Soil structure and also the plant's orientation are enhanced by the animal constituent of

---

* So-called 'terminator' seeds.

manure. Animals that chew the cud, such as cows, form a substrate with a high energy potential in the four-stomach digestive process. Cows barely extract consciousness forces from what they digest but leave these forces within it. Biodynamics considers that this benefits the plant and orientates it. That is why Demeter (biodynamic) farms usually rear cattle. Demeter is also the only organic certification that prohibits dehorning. Cows' horns are nevertheless important in biodynamic practice for a further characteristic reason. The produce we take from the ground in agriculture and cultivation withdraws not just substances but also forces from it. To reinvigorate it, Rudolf Steiner developed the so-called biodynamic preparations in the early 20s of the last century. In a way similar to the approach of anthroposophic medicine in developing organ remedies, organs – usually of the cow (e.g. the intestine) are used as a sheath for plant substance (camomile flowers in the case of cow intestines), and are buried over winter in the soil. In the spring the preparation is removed from the ground, the remaining intestinal material is disposed of, and the camomile flowers – which have undergone a subtle fermentation process – are added in small amounts to the compost, where they radiate fine energies. The primary goal here is revitalization of the earth: the human being nurtures the earth's specific connections with the cosmos, and consequently she gives us her produce, which can be further processed into food. According to Rudolf Steiner, all these measures should always remain in the living realm. Instead of 'dead' mineral fertilizers, stimulating forces and energies are used. All these measures aim at a kind of individualizing of the farm.

And this of course includes the human context as a decisive factor. Does sufficient awareness for particular processes develop on the farm, and can insight be translated into action? Social forms on each Demeter farm continually aim to meet this challenge, as does ongoing development of training concepts. Increasingly, relationships with people in the farm's surrounding locality are important too – such as customers and perhaps agricultural communities. An agriculture with future potential can only come into being as a joint venture.

To put it in a nutshell, one can say that the aims of biodynamic agriculture are to produce food which nourishes the whole human being and to practise an agriculture which enhances the earth's future. Many studies are now showing that the soil becomes more fertile through biodynamic methods, that plants grow in more strongly typical ways, and that biodynamic food can even help sustain emotional wellbeing. Ultimately, though, the context is the important thing: the place and value which food – in harmonious balance with other priorities – occupies in our lives.

Thus the specific qualities and characteristics of Demeter produce contribute to a form of nutrition which enhances vitality and promotes inner life. It is against this yardstick that we measure its value.

Nikolai Fuchs,
Agriculture Section at the Goetheanum

Sauces

18	Aubergine sauce
19	Avocado sauce
20	Béchamel sauce
21	Cream sauce
22	Curry sauce
23	Frothed carrot sauce
24	Genoese sauce
25	Herb vinegar sauce
26	Lentil sauce (dahl)
27	Mutabor sauce
28	Olive oil and lemon sauce
29	Paprika sauce
30	Pinenut sauce
31	Rice sauce
32	Salad dressing
33	Sauce piquante
34	Sauce ravigote
35	Sauce tartare
36	Sour cream and quark sauce
37	Squash and ginger sauce

Soups

40	Artichoke soup
41	Asparagus soup
42	Barley soup
43	Basel flour soup
44	Beetroot soup with sour cream
45	Butterballs
46	Caldo verde
47	Caraway soup
48	Caroline soup
49	Carrot soup
50	Chicory soup
51	Clear beetroot soup
52	Cold cucumber soup
53	Cream of celeriac soup
54	Croutons
55	Cucumber soup

Soups

Hors d'oeuvres

Hildegard of Bingen's herbal remedies

Hildegard of Bingen (1098–1179)

A Benedictine nun, she worked to reform ecclesiastical life in Germany through her prophetic writings, her letters, and travels (France, Lower Rhine, southern Germany). Hildegard was the first German mystic. She also wrote a treatise on nature, which mentions numerous folk remedies and treatment methods, and thus has medical significance.

Bibliography

Hildegard von Bingen: *Heilmittel.*

First complete and faithful translation, including all hand-written texts, translated by Marie-Louise Portmann.

Book 1: *Von den Pflanzen,* Basel 1982/1983.

Abbreviations

tbsp = tablespoon (15 ml)
tsp = teaspoon (5 ml)
g   = gram
kg   = kilogram
ml   = millilitre
l   = litre (1000 ml)

Wherever possible we use Demeter (biodynamic) – or at least organic – produce in the recipes.

Sbrinz cheese, used frequently in these recipes, is a hard Swiss cheese similar to Parmesan.

Tips

Herb bunches	Bay leaf, thyme, parsley stalks tied together with a slit leek. Depending on use can be augmented with rosemary, savoury, celery stalks and hyssop.
Bay onion	A bay leaf is fastened to half an onion with 1 or 2 cloves.
Stock garnish	Used in cooking grains, groats and vegetable hotpots 1 herb bunch 1 peeled carrot 1 parsley root or parsnip 1 bay onion optional: half a sautéed onion with peel
Roasted vegetables	Consists of diced onions, celery, carrots, possibly leek and garlic, to which is added a bay leaf, cloves, thyme and rosemary. The composition varies depending on use.
Herb pouch	Consists of various herbs and spices which, tied in a cloth, are cooked with the food and removed before serving. For cabbage, beans, stews, ragouts. Contents depending on use: allspice, mustard seeds, coriander, ginger, juniper, rosemary, caraway, fennel, peppercorns.

Unless stated, recipe quantities are for four persons

The recipes

Thyme
Thymus vulgaris

Thyme is warm and dry. And if someone adds to it good herbs and spices, its warmth and strength alleviates the corruption of this [abscess] pain. For where it is not spiced with other herbs and spices, its strength would penetrate the abscess with holes and not heal it when placed upon it. But also he who carries leprosy in himself should spice this herb with other good herbs and herb preparations, and thus he will soothe the leprosy, reducing through its warmth and strength the corruption of the leprosy, of whatever kind the leprosy may be. [The patient] should take the thyme with the earth of its roots, and let it simmer upon fire, and let him prepare with this a sweating bath, and also boil the thyme with the earth clinging thereto in the pot with water, and in this way make himself a bath; and this let him use often, and the warmth and dryness of the herb with the dry, heated earth, as stated before, will alleviate the bad juices, unless it should not please God. But if someone is plagued by palsy and twinges, and if he is as though gnawed and devoured by that disease which so plagues man's limbs, then let him take sage, and twice so much dwarf elder, and three times so much thyme as dwarf elder, and let him cook this in water, and then add deer tallow, and twice so much old fat, and let him make therewith an ointment, and, sitting beside the fire, rub this into the place where he has pain; and the warmth of the sage and the warmth of the dwarf elder, and of the thyme, in so far as the pleasantness of the heated and moderated water abets this, and also the warmth of the deer tallow and the warmth of the old fat, will alleviate the wrongly warm and wrongly cold pains produced by the above-named juices. [...]

Hildegard of Bingen

Aubergine sauce

Airy summer recipe

Preparation time	40 minutes

Ingredients		
	approx. 300 g	aubergine
	1	head of garlic
	10 sprigs	rosemary
	100 ml	vegetable stock
	100 ml	olive oil
		salt
		lemon juice
		Tabasco to taste

Preparation Wash the aubergines, peel them and cut into cubes. Cook the aubergine cubes with the peeled garlic and the rosemary in the vegetable stock until soft. Purée them in the mixer while still hot, and gradually add the olive oil. Pass through sieve and add salt, lemon juice and, where desired, Tabasco to taste. Variation: Prepare with sunflower oil and add sesame oil from roasted sesame to taste. A few drops are enough! If you cook 1 tbsp of pre-cooked rice with it, the sauce acquires a denser consistency.

> Check aubergines are shining and firm when buying

Sauces

Avocado sauce

Very delicate but short-lived

Preparation time	20 minutes	
Ingredients	1	avocado
	3 tbsp	lemon juice
	100 ml	olive oil
	½	chilli pepper, finely diced
	1 clove	garlic
	2 tbsp	onion, finely diced
	2 tbsp	vinegar (cider vinegar)
	1 tsp	dill, fresh, finely chopped
	½ tsp	pear purée
	1 pinch	salt

Preparation   Peel avocado, halve it, remove stone, and dice fruit. Mix immediately with lemon juice. Mix together the other ingredients and add salt to taste. You should prepare this sauce no more than 1–2 hours before use. Goes well with our celeriac terrine.

To ripen avocados, place them in warm position protected from light. It is best to wrap them in newspaper.

Béchamel sauce

Universal gravy

Preparation time	35 minutes	
Ingredients	30 g	semi-white flour, plain
	25 g	butter
	500 ml	milk, boiling hot
	1 small	bay onion
	½	bay leaf
		salt
		nutmeg

Preparation   Briefly sauté the flour in the melted butter and leave to cool a little. Pour on boiling milk and heat up while stirring. Add the onion and the bay leaf, and allow to simmer gently for 30 minutes. Add some more hot milk where needed. Season and strain.

Sauces

20

Cream sauce

Basis for several variations

Preparation time · 30 minutes

Ingredients
1	shallot
50 ml	kvass (bread drink)
25 g	butter
30 g	semi-white flour, plain
500–600 ml	vegetable stock
100 ml	cream
	salt
	nutmeg, freshly grated
	lemon juice

Preparation · Sauté the finely chopped shallot in the butter, pour in the kvass and boil down fully. Add the flour, briefly sauté and pour on the stock. Bring to the boil while stirring, and then allow to simmer gently for 30 minutes. Press through sieve, refine with the cream, and season.

> Variations: With fresh, chopped dill, with freshly grated horseradish, with fresh chervil, with sour cream instead of cream, with Gorgonzola, etc.

Curry sauce

Preparation time	35 minutes	
Ingredients	1 tbsp	butter
	50 g	onion
	1 tsp	ginger
	50 g	apple
	50 g	banana
	1 tbsp	curry powder
	1 tbsp (20 g)	rice flour
	300 ml	vegetable stock
	300 ml	cream
		salt
		lemon juice

Preparation   Peel onions, dice finely, and sauté in butter. Add the ginger and briefly sauté together. Slice apple and banana, add, and continue to cook. Shake the curry powder and rice flour over the mixture, briefly sauté and pour on vegetable stock. Bring back to boil and allow to simmer for 20 minutes. Mix together, pass through sieve and refine with cream. Season with salt and lemon juice.

Sauces

Frothed carrot sauce

Light vegetable-based sauce

Preparation time	40 minutes	
Ingredients	1	shallot or 1 small onion
	1 tbsp (20 g)	butter
	200 g (net weight)	carrots
	approx. 300 ml	vegetable stock
	1 tbsp	wholegrain rice, already cooked
	½	bay leaf
	4–5	coriander
		salt, herb salt
	1 tbsp	chervil, finely chopped
		lemon juice
	100 ml	cream, whipped until stiff

Preparation	Sauté the chopped shallot in the butter, and add the carrot cubes, bay leaf, coriander and the cooked rice. Pour on the vegetable stock and slowly simmer until soft. Season with salt and lemon juice. Shortly before serving, fold in the chervil and whipped cream.

Genoese sauce

Unique

Preparation time	20 minutes

Ingredients		
	100 g	butter
	50 ml	olive oil
	2–3 cloves	garlic
	2 tbsp	parsley (the flat-leaf type is more aromatic)
	1 bunch	basil
	75 g	Parmesan cheese, freshly grated
		salt

Preparation   Stir the butter and olive oil until light and frothy. Peel the garlic cloves and grate finely. Remove the stalks from the basil and parsley, and slice very finely or grind in a mortar. Add to the butter with the Parmesan and stir well. Season with salt. Serve cool with freshly cooked pasta.

Herb vinegar sauce

For cooked vegetable salads

Preparation   15 minutes
time

Ingredients   1 tbsp   parsley (the flat-leaf type is more aromatic)
               1 tsp   chervil
               2 tsp   tarragon
               ¼ tsp   salad burnet
               2 tsp   chives
               1 tsp   dill
               2 tbsp   onion
               250 ml   olive oil or sunflower oil
               100 ml   vinegar (cider vinegar or herb vinegar)
                             salt
                             pear purée

Preparation   Stir the finely cut herbs and onion with the vinegar and oil and season
               with salt and possibly pear purée. Stir well before using.

Lentil sauce (dahl)

Preparation time	30 minutes	
Ingredients	120 g	red lentils
	300 ml	water
	1 knife tip	turmeric
	1–2	green chilli peppers
	1 small	onion
	1 tsp	fresh ginger, finely chopped
	1 tsp	five-spice
	2 tbsp	clarified butter or olive oil
		salt
		lemon juice

Preparation   Mix together the washed and well-dried lentils with the finely chopped chilli peppers, the turmeric and water, and cook until soft. This takes about 20 minutes. In the meantime sauté the finely chopped onion in 1 tbsp clarified butter, and allow to go light golden-brown. Now add the ginger and sauté together for a further 2–3 minutes. Add this mixture to the lentils and bring back to the boil. Heat up the remaining clarified butter with the spice mix until the mustard seeds start to spit. Immediately add to the lentil mixture and season with salt and possibly lemon juice. If necessary dilute with a little vegetable stock.

Five-spice (Panch Poron) is a mixture of equal parts of: fennel seeds, black cumin, fenugreek, cumin and black mustard seeds. If you would prefer not to mix this up yourself you can buy it ready-made from Asian food shops.

Mutabor sauce

Cold sauce as accompaniment to breadcrumb-coated vegetables

Preparation time   20 minutes

Ingredients

2	eggs, hard-boiled
2 small	apples
1 small	onion
50 g	mustard, mild
100 ml	sour cream
	salt
	pear purée

Preparation   Peel the eggs and onion and chop finely. Grate the apple finely. Mix all ingredients together and season with salt and pear purée.

Olive oil and lemon sauce

Special sauce as accompaniment to millet bake

Preparation time	10 minutes

Ingredients	100 ml	olive oil: only the best olive oil will produce a good result
	2 tbsp	lemon juice, freshly squeezed
	2 tbsp	parsley, if possible the flat-leaf variety
		salt
		sea-salt or 'fleur du sel'

Preparation   Mix the olive oil and lemon juice well together, mix in the finely chopped parsley and season with salt. Important: do not prepare too long in advance, or the parsley will lose its colour.

Sauces

Paprika sauce

Strong to piquante

Preparation time	45 minutes	
Ingredients	1	shallot or onion
	1	red pepper, as ripe and full-fleshed as possible
	1 tbsp	olive oil or butter
	50 ml	kvass (bread drink)
	½ tbsp	paprika powder, delicate or noble sweet
	1 tbsp	wholegrain rice, already cooked
	200 ml	vegetable stock
	½	bay leaf
	1	clove
	1 small	chilli pepper
	5 sprigs	rosemary
		salt
		lemon juice
	1 tbsp	butter if needed

Preparation   Sauté the peeled, finely chopped shallot and seeded and sliced pepper in olive oil, add the paprika powder and roast mixture until it releases aromas. Pour in kvass and boil down fully. Add the rice and spices, except for the salt, and pour on stock. Bring back to the boil then cook on the lowest heat until soft. Mix for about 30 minutes, strain and season with salt, butter and lemon juice.

Chilli peppers are milder if you remove the seeds

Pinenut sauce

Pesto variation

Preparation time	10 minutes

Ingredients

1 bunch	basil, just the leaves
2–3 cloves	garlic
100 ml	olive oil, best quality
50 g	pinenuts
100 ml	vegetable stock, hot
50 g	Parmesan cheese, freshly grated
	salt
	lemon juice

Preparation
Roast the pinenuts in a dry pan until they go brown in places. Mix in the coarsely chopped basil leaves, garlic, pinenuts and the olive oil, slowly pouring on the hot vegetable stock at the same time, and finally add the Parmesan. If necessary, dilute with stock. Season with salt and lemon juice (optional).

Sauces

Rice sauce

Basic sauce like cream sauce, but lighter

Preparation
time

about 45 minutes

Ingredients

1	shallot
50 ml	kvass (bread drink)
75 g	wholegrain rice, already cooked and soft
600 ml	vegetable stock, cold
½	bay leaf
1	clove
20–50 g	butter or olive oil, cream, etc.
	salt

Preparation

Finely chop the shallot and boil down with the kvass. Add the rice, the vegetable stock and the spices. Bring to the boil, then turn the heat right down and simmer under light cover until the rice has almost dissolved. Press through a sieve (mixing together first may be necessary). While mixing, cold pieces of butter or oil can be added. Season. Use like cream sauce. You can also leave out the kvass and shallot, and then season with lemon juice.

Salad dressing

The Lukas Klinik's salad dressing

Preparation time	10 minutes	
Ingredients	1–2 tsp	mustard
	1 tsp	nutmeg
	150 ml	lemon juice, freshly squeezed
	400 ml	sunflower oil or olive oil
	400 ml	fermented milk (sour milk), yoghurt or buttermilk
	1–2 tsp	salt, herb salt as desired
	1 tsp	horseradish, freshly grated (only in months with 'r')
		fresh herbs according to taste, in winter also dried herbs
	a little	pear purée

Preparation

Put the nutmeg, mustard, salt, lemon juice, fermented milk and horse-radish in an electric mixer and blend. Slowly add the oil as you do so. If desired, add a little pear purée. Store the dressing in the fridge, and add fresh herbs daily to the salad.

Herb selection: dill, parsley, chives, salad burnet, tarragon, chervil, hyssop. Use no more than 2–3 herbs at one time. If you only use half the fermented milk, the dressing becomes very thick and can be used instead of mayonnaise.

Sauce piquante

Instead of tomato sauce

Preparation time	90 minutes	
Ingredients	2 tbsp	olive oil
	50 g (net weight)	onion
	50 g	carrots
	50 g	celeriac
	50 g	white cabbage
	50 g	leek
	½ bunch	parsley, just the stems
	1 small	bay leaf
	1	clove
	1 small	chilli pepper
	1 tbsp	paprika powder, delicate or noble sweet
	30 g	rice – risotto rice is good for binding
	500 ml	water or vegetable stock
		lemon juice
		pear purée
		salt
	50 ml	cream

Preparation   Cut onions, carrots, celeriac, cabbage and leek into 1 cm cubes, and sauté in the oil until the vegetables are golden brown. This takes about 20 minutes. Be careful that nothing burns, otherwise the sauce will be bitter. Now add the paprika powder and briefly sauté with the other ingredients. Pour in the water and add the rice, parsley stalks and spices. Bring to the boil and allow to simmer gently for 30 minutes under lightly sealed lid. Mix the sauce and press through sieve. Where necessary dilute a little. Season and refine with cream.

Sauce ravigote

Variation on the herb vinegar sauce

Preparation time   10 minutes

Ingredients   200 ml   herb vinegar sauce
               1 tbsp   capers, finely chopped
               2–3 tbsp   gherkins, finely chopped

Preparation   Mix the capers and gherkins into the herb vinegar sauce and season again.

Sauces

34

Sauce tartare

Accompaniment to boiled vegetables (artichokes, avocado)

Preparation time	15 minutes	
Ingredients	200 ml	salad dressing as in this book, with half quantity of fermented milk
	1	egg, hard-boiled and finely chopped
	2	pickled gherkins, finely chopped
	1 tbsp	chives, finely chopped
	1 tbsp	capers, finely chopped
	1 tbsp	quark
	2 tbsp	parsley, finely chopped
		salt
		pepper

Preparation   Mix the salad dressing with the other ingredients and season with salt and a little freshly milled pepper.

Sour-cream and quark sauce

A good accompaniment to boiled artichokes

Preparation time	15 minutes

Ingredients		
	250 g	quark, full-fat
	100 ml	sour cream or crème fraîche
	1 tsp	mustard
	1 tsp	dill
	1 tbsp	parsley
	2–3	pickled gherkins
	1 tsp	capers
		salt
		pear purée or honey
	1	egg (optional)
		Tabasco

Preparation	Mix the quark well with the sour cream and the mustard. Finely chop the herbs, the pickled gherkins and the capers and mix into the quark mass. Season with salt, pear purée and possibly Tabasco.

A finely chopped hard-boiled egg makes the sauce still richer.

Squash and ginger sauce

Goes well with exotic dishes

Preparation time	40 minutes	
Ingredients	1 tbsp	butter or olive oil
	1 tbsp	ginger, finely chopped
	1 tbsp	shallot, finely chopped
	300 g (net weight)	squash, roughly cubed
	1 small	bay leaf
	1	clove
	1 tbsp	wholegrain rice, already cooked
	100 ml	vegetable stock
	1 small	chilli pepper (optional)
	1–2 tbsp	butter, olive oil or sesame oil
		lemon juice
		salt

Preparation	Sauté the finely chopped shallot and the ginger in the butter. Add the pumpkin, spices, rice and vegetable stock, cover lightly with lid and simmer until soft. Mix and at the same time add the oil or butter. Press through a sieve and season with salt and lemon juice. You can also substitute herbs, e.g. tarragon, instead of ginger.

Use firm-fleshed squash, e.g. Potimarron ('Hokaido' squash) or 'Butternut'.

Parsley
Petroselinum crispum

Parsley is strong by nature and has greater warmth than coldness in it, and it grows from the wind and the moisture. And it is better for man to eat it raw, not cooked. And once eaten it assuages fevers of the type that do not convulse but only lightly affect him. In the human spirit, however, it engenders gravity. But he who has pains in the heart, or spleen, or in the side, should cook parsley in wine and add thereto a little vinegar and sufficient honey, and then let him strain it through a cloth, and drink it often, and it will heal him. But he, too, who is sick in the stomach, should take parsley and twice as much fennel, and as much soapwort as parsley, and let him make therewith a mixture to which he is to add butter or deer tallow and roasted salt, and thus cooked let him eat this often. But he too who eats leek and has pains therefrom should eat parsley straight away, and his pain will be less. And he who suffers from a stone, let him take parsley and add thereto a third portion of saxifrage, and this let him cook in wine, and sieve it through a cloth, and let him then drink this in a sweating bath. And (let him) again take parsley and add thereto a third portion of saxifrage and cook this in water, and in this same sweating bath let him pour this water over the painful stones. And let him do this often, and it will go better for him. He too who is plagued by palsy, let him take parsley and fennel in equal portions, and a little less sage. And these herbs let him crush together gently in a mortar, adding thereto olive oil infused with rose, and let him place this where he has ague, and bind upon it a cloth. And he who has soft flesh and, as consequence of excessive drinking suffers gout in one of his limbs, let him take parsley and four times as much rue, and roast these in a pot with olive oil or, should he have no oil, let him roast it with goat tallow; and these warm herbs let him place where he has pains, and bind a cloth over, and it will go better for him.

Hildegard of Bingen

Artichoke soup

Delicate cream of vegetable soup

Preparation time	1 hour	
Ingredients	2	globe artichokes
	1	bay onion
	1	herb pouch
	400 ml	vegetable stock
	400 ml	water
	40 g	rice flour
	100 ml	water
	100 ml	cream
	1	egg yolk
		herb salt
	1 bunch	chives

Preparation — Cook the well-washed artichokes with the bay onion and the herb pouch in a little, lightly salted water until soft. Take off the leaves and remove the thistly hair from the button bottom, and dice. Scrape the thick part from the larger leaves. Measure out 400 ml of the cooking water and mix with the leaf flesh. Add to the vegetable stock and bring to the boil. Whisk the rice flour with the cold water and stir into the boiling liquid. Allow to simmer for 25 minutes. Mix together the egg yolk and cream, pass through sieve into soup and stir. Heat while stirring, but do not allow to boil again. Season, put the cubed artichoke bottom into the soup, sprinkle with chives, and serve.

If you use Italian artichokes, you can include the stem.

Soups

Asparagus soup

Now spring's really arrived!

Preparation time	45 minutes	
Ingredients	300 g	white asparagus
	1 l	vegetable stock
	20 g	butter
	50 g	onions
	25 g (1 tbsp)	flour or rice flour
	100 ml	cream
	1 tsp	chervil, finely chopped

Preparation — Wash the asparagus and peel the stems. Put the peelings into a pot with the cold vegetable stock and simmer for 20 minutes (asparagus stock). Drain. Cut the asparagus tips to lengths of about 3 cm, cook them until soft in a little asparagus stock, and chop small. Cut the remaining pieces into slices and sauté with the finely chopped onion in the butter. Sprinkle on the flour, stir well and pour on the sieved asparagus stock. Bring to the boil while stirring and simmer for 20 minutes on a low heat. Blend and pass through a sieve. Add the cream and season with salt and a pinch of sugar if desired. Add the finely chopped tips to the soup and sprinkle with chervil.

The soup becomes more delicate if you whip the cream and fold it in shortly before serving.

Barley soup

Preparation time	1 hour + soaking time	
Ingredients	1 tbsp	olive oil or butter
	1 clove	garlic
	1 small	onion
	1 small sprig	thyme
	½ tsp	rosemary, finely chopped
	½	bay leaf
	40 g	barley, soaked for 1–2 hours in water
	80 g	cubed vegetables: carrot, celery, leek, parsley root
	approx. 1 l	vegetable stock, cold
		salt, herb salt as desired
		nutmeg, freshly grated
	½ tbsp	parsley, chives or chervil

Preparation Chop the garlic and onion into small pieces and sauté with the herbs in oil or butter. Add the vegetable cubes, briefly sauté, then add the barley with the soaking water. Fill pot with the vegetable stock and bring to the boil. Cook for about 30 minutes on low heat, until soft. Season and serve with chopped herbs. Also tastes very good with oats!

Basel flour soup

Traditional on Shrove Tuesday

Preparation time — about 2 hours

Ingredients		
100 g	semi-white flour, plain	
40 g	clarified butter	
350 g	onions	
1.5 l	vegetable stock	
100 ml	red wine	
50 g	Sbrinz cheese, grated	
	salt	
1 pinch	nutmeg, freshly grated	

Preparation — Roast the flour in an oven until brown, stirring frequently. Leave to cool and sieve. Chop the onions finely and sauté slowly in the clarified butter until golden brown. Add the roasted flour and mix well. Add the hot vegetable stock and bring to the boil while stirring. Add the red wine and simmer for at least 1 hour, removing froth now and then. Season. Serve the Sbrinz cheese separately. Croutons go very well with this.

Beetroot soup with sour cream

Russian feel

Preparation time	1–1½ hours	
Ingredients	50 g	onions
	50 g	carrots
	100 g	white cabbage
	1 tbsp (20 g)	butter
	1 tbsp	semi-white flour, plain
	1 l	vegetable stock
	1	bay leaf
	1	clove
		vinegar (cider vinegar) as desired
		pear purée, as desired
	200 g	beetroots, cooked, peeled and cubed
	100 ml	sour cream
	1 tbsp	dill or parsley, finely chopped
		salt

Preparation — Chop the onions small. Dice the carrots and white cabbage and sauté with the onions in the butter. Add bay leaf, clove and flour, briefly sauté them too, then pour on vegetable stock and simmer for 30 minutes. Add the beetroot to the soup, season, and allow to draw for 5 minutes, possibly seasoning further. Mix together the sour cream with the dill and salt and serve separately.

Soups

Butterballs

To add to soups (10 portions)

Preparation time	30 minutes + 1 hour to cool	
Ingredients	50 g	butter, at room temperature
	2	eggs, at room temperature
	75 g	breadcrumbs
	1 tsp	parsley, finely chopped
	1 pinch	nutmeg, freshly grated
	½ tsp	salt

Preparation   Stir the butter with the salt until light and frothy. Carefully beat in the eggs. Mix in the breadcrumbs and the parsley, and season with nutmeg and salt. Once the mass is solid, take small scoops with a teaspoon and form hazelnut-sized balls. Cook for 10–12 minutes in simmering water.

Caldo verde

Portuguese potato soup

Preparation time	1 hour	
Ingredients	2 tbsp	olive oil
	100 g	onions
	400 g	potatoes, roast
	1	bay leaf
	1	clove
	1.2 l	vegetable stock
		salt
		pepper
	80 g	cabbage, kohlrabi leaves or broccoli

Preparation   Cut the peeled onion into strips and lightly sauté in the oil, without letting them change colour. Add the roughly cubed potatoes and spices. Pour on the stock and simmer for 25 minutes until soft. Blend and season. Cut the cabbage leaves into very thin strips, briefly blanche them in salted water, strain and add to the finished soup.

The original version uses 'Butterkohl' (open-headed golden Savoy), which is however hard to find.

Soups

Caraway soup

Cream of barley soup

Preparation time	40 minutes

Ingredients		
	1–2 tbsp	caraway
	40 g	barley
	1 pinch	thyme
	½ tsp	marjoram
	1 l	vegetable stock, cold
	100 ml	cream
	1	egg yolk
		salt
	½ tbsp	parsley, finely chopped

Preparation	Finely mill the barley and caraway, and dry roast until aromas start to be released. Add thyme and marjoram, pour on the vegetable stock, bring to the boil and allow to simmer for 25 minutes. Mix together the cream and egg yolk and pass through a sieve, stirring into soup. Heat while continuing to stir, but do not allow to boil again. Strain the soup, season and serve sprinkled with the parsley.

Caroline soup

Rice and almond soup

Preparation time	30 minutes	

Ingredients	30 g	butter
	50 g	rice flour
	800 ml	vegetable stock
	1	egg yolk
	50 ml	cream
	100 ml	almond milk (1 tbsp almond paste stirred with water)
	60 g	rice, cooked
	1 tbsp	chervil, finely chopped
		salt

Preparation
Sauté the rice flour in the butter, pour on the vegetable stock, bring to the boil and simmer gently for 25 minutes. Mix egg yolk and cream, and stir into the soup. Heat while stirring, but do not allow to boil again. Strain, season, and refine with the almond milk. Add the cooked rice and serve sprinkled with chervil.

Soups

Carrot soup

Preparation time

40 minutes

Ingredients	1 tbsp	olive oil or butter
	30 g	leek
	30 g	celeriac
	30 g	onions
	350 g	carrots
	½	bay leaf
	1	clove
	1 sprig	thyme, tarragon or oregano
	1 l	vegetable stock
	100 ml	cream
		salt
	½ tbsp	parsley or chervil
		croutons (see recipe)

Preparation   Finely chop the onions, leek and celeriac and sauté in oil. Coarsely cube the carrots and add to the other vegetables with the spices. Briefly continue to sauté, pour on the vegetable stock and simmer half covered. Blend and pass through sieve. Add the cream and season with salt. Sprinkle with finely chopped herbs. Serve the croutons separately.

Chicory soup

To stimulate the appetite

Preparation time	40 minutes, including cooking time

Ingredients		
	2	chicory (Belgian, Brussels)
	1 tbsp (20 g)	butter or olive oil
	800 ml	vegetable stock
	40 g	rice flour or wheat flour
	100 ml	cream
	1	egg yolk
		lemon juice
		herb salt
		nutmeg, freshly grated
		parsley, finely chopped

Preparation   Cut the chicory into fine strips, wash it quickly in water slightly acidified with lemon juice, and allow to dry. Heat the butter and sauté the chicory in it until it goes a golden brown colour. Pour on 700 ml of vegetable stock and bring to the boil. Whisk the flour with the rest of the cold vegetable stock and stir into the soup. Allow to simmer for 20 minutes on a low heat. Whisk the egg yolk with the cream and pass through a sieve into the soup, then slowly heat while stirring carefully. Do not allow to boil again! If necessary dilute with a little vegetable stock. Season and serve with chopped parsley.

Soups

Clear beetroot soup

Distinctive aroma

Preparation time	1 hour

Ingredients		
	75 g	red lentils
	150 g	celeriac, topped and tailed
	500 g	beetroots, topped and tailed
	1 l	vegetable stock, cold
		salt
		raspberry or balsamic vinegar
		Tabasco (optional)

Preparation   Wash the lentils. Cook until soft in sufficient water, pour off and rinse in cold water. Cut the celeriac into fine strips (julienne), cook in salt water until just soft, and rinse in cold water. Peel the beetroot, finely grate and heat with the cold stock. Bring to the boil, then place lid on and leave to simmer for 15 minutes on the lowest heat. Strain, season with salt, vinegar and Tabasco if desired. Add lentils and celeriac. Note: the colour will be lost if the soup is kept warm for a long time.

Cold cucumber soup

Quick and good

Preparation time	20 minutes

Ingredients		
	800 g	cucumber
	4 cloves	garlic
	200 ml	sour cream
	600 ml	sour milk or yoghurt
	2 tbsp	olive oil
	1 tbsp	dill, finely chopped
		herb salt
		cider vinegar or lemon juice
		Tabasco

Preparation Wash and peel the cucumbers and if necessary remove seeds. Cut 100 g of cucumber into small cubes and place in fridge. Coarsely cube the rest of the cucumber and blend with the peeled garlic, olive oil, yoghurt and sour cream. Add piquant seasoning with salt, herbs, vinegar and Tabasco. Leave to cool for 1–2 hours, add the small cucumber cubes, and serve.

Soups

Cream of celeriac soup

Distinctive aroma

Preparation time · 40 minutes

Ingredients		
	1 tbsp (25 g)	butter
	50 g	onions or shallots
	200 g (net weight)	celeriac
	½	bay leaf
	1	clove
	1 small	chilli pepper
	1 tbsp (20 g)	risotto rice, Arborio binds well
	1 l	vegetable stock
	50 ml	cream
	1	egg yolk
		salt, herb salt as desired
	½ tbsp	chervil or parsley

Preparation · Finely chop the onions and sauté in the butter. Add the diced celeriac, the rice and the spices, and briefly sauté together. Pour in the vegetable stock and simmer until soft. Blend and strain. Mix the egg yolk together with the cream and pass through a sieve into the soup while stirring. Heat while continuing to stir, but do not allow to boil again. Season with salt and serve sprinkled with the chopped parsley or chervil.

Croutons

To add interest to cream of vegetable soups

Preparation time   15 minutes

Ingredients	2 slices	toast, white or wholemeal
	½ tsp	paprika powder, possibly add some chilli
	1 tbsp	olive oil
	1 clove	garlic, finely grated
	two drops	vinegar (cider vinegar)

Preparation   Cube the bread, mix well with the spices and oil, and bake in the oven until golden brown. Serve separately.

Soups

Cucumber soup

Refreshing summer soup

Preparation time	35 minutes	
Ingredients	1	cucumber
	20 g	butter or olive oil
	30 g	flour
	800 ml	vegetable stock
	½	bay leaf
	1	clove
	1 small	chilli pepper (optional)
	2–3 sprigs	tarragon
	100 ml	sour cream
	½ tbsp	dill
		salt

Preparation: Peel the cucumber and roughly cube. Cut a quantity of 3 tablespoons into very small cubes and leave to one side. Sauté the remaining cucumber cubes in the butter, add the spices, briefly continue to sauté, and sprinkle on the flour. Pour on the vegetable stock and simmer until soft. Blend and strain. Season and add the sour cream and the finely chopped dill. Sauté the small cucumber cubes in a little butter and add to the soup.

Green spelt soup

Green spelt is spelt harvested when semi-ripe and then dried over a wood fire

Preparation time	30 minutes

Ingredients		
	50 g	green spelt flour, freshly milled
	20 g	butter
	1 l	vegetable stock, cold
	50 ml	cream
	1	egg yolk
		salt, herb salt as desired

Preparation   Sauté the green spelt flour in the butter, pour in the vegetable stock, bring to the boil and simmer for 20 minutes. Mix together the egg yolk and the cream, and pass through sieve into the soup. Heat while stirring, but do not bring back to the boil. Season with salt and marjoram, and serve sprinkled with parsley.

Slight variation: Dissolve the green spelt flour in 200 ml of the vegetable stock, and mix into the boiling vegetable stock. Then continue as above.

Soups

Hungarian pepper soup

All possible variations, from mild to sharp and fiery

Preparation time	40 minutes	
Ingredients	75 g (net weight)	pepper, red
	½	bay leaf
	1 sprig	thyme
	1 tbsp	butter, olive oil is also good
	800 ml	vegetable stock
	80 g	rice, cooked
	100 ml	cream, milk can also be used
	1 tsp	cornflour (maize starch)
	1 pinch	nutmeg, freshly grated
		Tabasco (optional)
	1 tbsp	parsley, finely chopped
		salt

Preparation
Cut the pepper into fine strips and slowly sauté in the fat until it starts to roast. Now add the bay leaf and the thyme and pour on the vegetable stock. Bring to the boil and simmer for 20 minutes on a low heat. After 15 minutes add the cooked rice and continue to simmer. Mix the cornflour to a smooth paste with the milk or the cream, stir into the soup and bring back to the boil. Season with nutmeg, Tabasco and salt. Serve sprinkled with parsley.

Leek soup

Preparation time	35 minutes	
Ingredients	350 g (net weight)	leeks (only use the white parts)
	1 tbsp (25 g)	butter
	1 tbsp (15 g)	flour, where desired also with oatmeal or rice flour
	½	bay leaf
	1 pinch	marjoram
	½ tsp	mustard seeds
	1 l	vegetable stock
	1 pinch	nutmeg, freshly grated
		lemon juice to taste
		salt
	½ tbsp	parsley, finely chopped
	100 ml	cream (optional)

Preparation   Halve the leeks lengthways, wash well and cut into fine strips. Heat the butter and sauté the leeks well on a low heat (10 minutes). Add the flour and the spices, briefly sauté them too, and pour on the vegetable stock. Bring to the boil and simmer for 25 minutes. Season and serve sprinkled with parsley.

> The soup gains added finesse and richness by the addition of a little cream.

Soups

Lentil soup

Greetings from Esau

Preparation time	1 hour + soaking time

Ingredients		
	100 g	lentils, brown
	¼ tsp	turmeric
	1 l	water, or lightly salted vegetable stock
	1 tbsp (20 g)	butter
	2 tbsp	carrots, diced
	2 tbsp	leeks, the green part, diced
	2 tbsp	parsley, finely chopped
	1 tsp	savoury, dried
	1 small	chilli pepper (optional)
		soya sauce to taste
		vinegar (cider vinegar)
		salt
		vegetable stock to dilute

Preparation   Soak the washed lentils overnight. Pour away the soaking water and cook the lentils in 1 l of water or the vegetable stock, together with the turmeric and the chilli pepper, until soft. Sauté the diced vegetables and the herbs in the butter, blend the lentils with the cooking water and strain into the vegetables, possibly diluting with vegetable stock. Bring to the boil while stirring and allow to simmer gently for 20 minutes. Season.

There is no need to strain red (peeled) lentils.

Linseed soup

Preparation   30 minutes
time

Ingredients   2 tbsp   linseed
                1 tsp   caraway
                40 g   barley flour
                1 tbsp (20 g)   butter
                1 l   vegetable stock
                1 tsp   lovage, fresh, or ½ tsp dried
                50 ml   cream
                50 ml   yoghurt
                1   egg yolk
                1 tsp   parsley, finely chopped
                                  salt

Preparation   Roast the linseed and caraway without fat until aromas are released.
                Place on a plate to cool then grind in a coffee mill or processor. Sauté the
                barley flour in the butter, add the caraway, linseed and lovage, stir well
                and pour on the vegetable stock. Bring to the boil and simmer gently for
                20 minutes. Mix together cream, yoghurt and egg yolk and stir into the
                soup. Heat while stirring but do not bring back to the boil. Strain, season
                and serve with the parsley.

Soups

Minestrone

Preparation time	1 hour	
Ingredients	1–2 cloves	garlic, finely chopped
	2 leaves	sage, finely chopped
	2 tbsp	olive oil
	50 g	onions, finely chopped
	100 g	leeks
	100 g	carrots
	100 g	Savoy cabbage
	50 g	celeriac
	100 g	potatoes
	100 g	squash or zucchini
	1 tbsp	rice
	30 g	elbow macaroni*
	2–3 leaves	basil, finely cut
	1 tbsp	parsley, finely chopped
		salt, herb salt as desired
	1.25 l	vegetable stock
	50 g	Parmesan cheese, freshly grated

Preparation   Finely chop the vegetables. Lightly warm the oil, add the garlic and the sage and sauté a little so that the oil soaks up the aromas. Add the onions and sauté. Now add the rest of the vegetables and the rice. Sauté these too, and then pour on the vegetable stock. Bring to the boil and simmer for about 40 minutes. Add the pasta 10 minutes before the soup is ready. Season and sprinkle on the basil and parsley. Serve the Parmesan separately.

---

* A small type of pasta, known in Switzerland as 'Hörnli'.

Nettle soup

Light spring soup

Preparation time	40 minutes

Ingredients	40 g	barley flour
	20 g	butter
	1 l	vegetable stock, hot
	100 g	nettle tips
	100 ml	cream
		herb salt

Preparation   Wash the freshly picked nettles, briefly blanch and quickly cool in cold water. Cut finely. Now sauté the barley flour in the butter, leave to cool a little, pour on the hot stock and leave to simmer for 25–30 minutes, stirring occasionally. Add the nettles in the last ten minutes. Refine with the cream and season with herb salt.

> A variation is to use wild garlic leaves and oatmeal. The flour can also be mixed with just a little cold stock (less fat).

Noodles

To add to soups (10 portions)

Preparation time	15 minutes	
Ingredients	150 g	semi-white flour, plain, if desired 'middlings' (pasta flour)
	1	egg, large
	1 pinch	nutmeg, freshly grated
	½ tsp	herb salt
Preparation	Knead the ingredients together into a solid dough, and make fine noodles by passing through a noodle maker (Bircher grater).* Allow to cook in simmering water for 3–4 minutes.	

---

* These can be ordered from Switzerland via the internet. The Swiss name is 'Bircherraffel'.

Passatelli

To add to soups (10 portions)

Preparation time | 20 minutes + 15 minutes waiting

Ingredients
60 g	Parmesan cheese, freshly grated
75 g	breadcrumbs
25 g	semi-white flour, plain
2	eggs
1 pinch	salt, herb salt as desired
1 pinch	paprika powder
1 pinch	nutmeg, freshly grated

Preparation | Mix all ingredients well, and season with the spices and salt. Leave for 15 minutes. Press through a sieve into simmering salted water, and as soon as the passatelli rise to the surface take them out, cool them in cold water and drain in a sieve. To serve, warm in the hot vegetable stock. One can also directly cook the mass in the simmering stock, which then becomes somewhat cloudy.

Pea soup

Preparation time	1 hour	

Ingredients	100 g	peas, dried green peas
	50 g (net weight)	celeriac root
	50 g (net weight)	carrots
	1 tbsp (20 g)	butter
		salt, herb salt
	1 pinch	marjoram
	1 pinch	savoury
	1 pinch	nutmeg, freshly grated
	1 pinch	chilli powder (optional)
	½ tbsp	parsley or chives
	100 ml	cream
	1 knife-tip	turmeric

Preparation   Leave the peas to soak for several hours or overnight. Pour away the water and cook the peas in 800 ml of (lightly salted) water and the turmeric. In the meantime, cut the carrots and the celeriac into fine cubes and sauté with the marjoram and savoury in the butter. Pour on 200 ml of vegetable stock and cook until soft. Blend the peas and add to the soup. Bring back to the boil and possibly dilute with some vegetable stock. Fold in the cream and season. Serve with the chopped parsley.

Potage Ivanka

Preparation   10 minutes
time

Ingredients   800 ml   vegetable stock, strongly seasoned
                 1   egg
                 50 ml   water
                 50 ml   cream
                 1 tsp (5 g)   semi-white flour
                 2 tbsp   herbs, finely chopped (parsley, chervil, lovage,
                                           etc.)
                                           herb salt
                                           nutmeg

Preparation   Bring the vegetable stock to the boil. Blend the egg finely with water,
                 cream, flour and the herbs, and stir into the boiling stock. Bring back to
                 the boil briefly while stirring, and season with herb salt.

Soups

Pumpkin soup

A variation on the theme

Preparation time	45 minutes	
Ingredients	100 g (net weight)	celeriac
	100 g	leeks
	100 g	onions
	400 g	pumpkin
	20 g	butter
	1 tbsp	rice
	800 ml	vegetable stock
	100 ml	cream
		salt
	½ tsp	curry powder, or more depending on taste
	1 tbsp	chives

Preparation   Finely cut the celeriac, leeks and onions and sauté in the butter. Add the cubed pumpkin and the rice, briefly sauté them as well, then pour on the stock. Bring to the boil and simmer for 25–30 minutes until soft. Blend and strain. Refine with the cream and season with salt and curry powder. Serve with the finely chopped chives.

> The curry taste becomes stronger if you sauté the curry powder with the vegetables.

Semolina balls

To add to soups (10 portions)

Preparation time   30 minutes + 20 minutes waiting time

Ingredients

40 g	butter, at room temperature
80 g	semolina (durum wheat), wholegrain
1	egg
1 pinch	nutmeg, freshly grated
1 pinch	marjoram
½ tsp	salt, herb salt as desired

Preparation   Mix together the butter, semolina and egg and season with the spices. Leave for about 20 minutes. Form small balls with two teaspoons, and cook for 15–20 minutes in simmering water.

Soups

Semolina soup

Simple and good

Preparation time	30 minutes

Ingredients		
	100 g	vegetables, various kinds, cut into tiny cubes
	50 g	semolina (durum wheat), oat flakes or maize-meal
	20 g	butter
	1 l	vegetable stock
	1 pinch	thyme
	1 pinch	nutmeg, freshly grated
		salt
	1 tbsp	chervil, parsley, chives or lovage

Preparation   Sauté the semolina in the butter, add the vegetables and briefly sauté them too, and pour on the vegetable stock. Add the thyme, bring to the boil and simmer for 20 minutes. Season with salt and nutmeg, and serve with finely chopped herbs.

> Variation: Roast the semolina without fat until golden brown, then continue as above.

Vegetable stock

Basis for many soups and sauces

Preparation   about 1 hour
time

Ingredients   250 ml   cold water
                1 kg   vegetables, washed and cut small
                1   bay leaf
                2   cloves
                ½ tsp   mustard seeds
                ½ tsp   lovage
                1 bunch   parsley, possibly only the stalks
                1 sprig   thyme, possibly only the stalks
                                    soya sauce
                                    salt

Preparation   Place the washed and finely cut vegetables and left-overs such as carrot
                peel, parsley stalks and roots, celery, leeks, garlic, onions, parsnips,
                a bay leaf, a sprig of thyme, cloves, lovage and mustard seeds in a
                saucepan of cold water and bring to the boil. Allow to simmer on low
                heat for about an hour. Strain and season with salt and possibly soya
                sauce. It can be stored with a lid for several days in the fridge.

Soups

Zucchini soup with pesto

Very delicate

Preparation time	30 minutes

Ingredients		
	300 g	small, young courgettes (zucchetti)
	1 small	onion
	120 g	rice, risotto rice
	150 ml	vegetable stock
	2 tbsp	olive oil
	4 tbsp	pesto
	2–3	slices of white bread (toasting bread)
	30 g	butter
	30 g	Parmesan cheese, freshly grated

Preparation Wash the courgettes and cut into 1 cm cubes. Dice the onion and sauté in the olive oil. Add the courgettes and the rice and briefly sauté together. Pour on the vegetable stock and cook until soft. Season. Stir the butter and the cheese together until light and fluffy, and spread on the slices of bread. Briefly bake au gratin in the oven, removing before they colour. Cut the bread into squares and serve these and the pesto separately as accompaniment.

Lovage
Levisticum officinale

Lovage is of moderate warmth. And if one eats it raw it renders man open and fluid, and thus reveals his nature. But if someone should eat it cooked without other herbs, it would render him heavy and lacklustre in mind and body. But when cooked with other herbs and eaten, it will do no great harm to whoever eats it. And if a person suffers from pains in the glands of the throat, so that the throat vessels are swollen, then let him take lovage and somewhat more ground ivy, and let him cook these together in water. After the water has been poured away, let him place this warmly around his throat since his throat vessels are too much extended, and he will be cured. And if someone has a cough in the chest, so that he first begins to feel pain therein, then let him take lovage and sage in equal portions, and twice as much fennel as these two, and let him place these in good wine until the wine takes up their taste and then, after removing these herbs, let him warm this wine and drink it warm after eating, until he is cured. If however the coughing is moderate, then let a person drink this potion not warmed, as the pain is mild. If the pain is strong, however, he should drink the wine warmed, so that this pain be more pleasantly assuaged. [...]

Hildegard of Bingen

American salad

Preparation time	20 minutes

Ingredients		
	4 slices	pineapple
	150 g	cream cheese (California)
	1 tsp	chervil, finely chopped
		Tabasco, to taste
	1	egg, hard-boiled
	1 tbsp	salad dressing (see recipe), spicily seasoned
	8	lettuce leaves
	1 pinch	paprika powder, noble sweet
	1 stalk	parsley

Preparation   Stir the cream cheese with the finely chopped herbs until smooth, and season with Tabasco. Put one slice of pineapple on two lettuce leaves (x 4), and squirt the cream cheese with a piping bag in rosette shape on the pineapple slices. Peel and quarter the egg. Place the quarters on the cream cheese, dribble on a little salad dressing, sprinkle with paprika powder and garnish with the parsley.

Asparagus with vinaigrette dressing

A taste for the spring

Preparation time	40 minutes including cooking time

Ingredients		
	1.5 kg	asparagus, white stems, very fresh
		salt
	1 tsp	olive oil
	200 ml	herb vinegar dressing made with the best olive oil

Preparation
Wash and peel the asparagus. Cook until soft in salty water with 1 tsp olive oil. Remove and place on a platter. Pour on the vinaigrette dressing and serve lukewarm.

Blériot salad

Spicy hors d'oeuvre

Preparation time	25 minutes + cooking time for beetroot

Ingredients		
	350 g	beetroot, cooked and peeled, weighed
	½ (approx. 500 g)	pineapple
	100 g	Emmental cheese
	100 ml	salad dressing (see recipe p. 32)
	1–2 tbsp	sour cream
	1 tsp	parsley, finely chopped, or dill
	1 tbsp	vinegar (cider vinegar)
		lettuce leaves to garnish
		salt

Preparation	Cut the beetroot into stick-lengths and marinade with the vinegar and a little salt. Likewise cut the pineapple and Emmenthal cheese into sticks, and add to the beetroot. Add the salad dressing and the sour cream and mix well. Season. Arrange on lettuce leaves and serve sprinkled with parsley. Also tastes good with fresh dill.

Blini

Russian pancakes

Preparation time	30 minutes + fermenting time

Ingredients		
	125 g	buckwheat flour
	125 g	wheat flour
	10 g	fresh yeast
	300 ml	milk
	1	egg
	50 ml	cream, whipped
		salt
		nutmeg
		marjoram

Preparation	Dissolve the yeast in the milk and mix with the flour. Cover and leave for one hour to ferment. Separate the yolk from the egg white and add. Whip the egg white until stiff and fold into the mixture with the cream. Season with the spices and salt. Possibly dilute a little with milk. Heat a little clarified butter in a pan and cook small pancakes in it. Serve with sour cream, hard-boiled eggs and pickled gherkin.

Crispi cocktail

Refreshing hors d'oeuvre

Preparation time   30 minutes

Ingredients
2	pears
2	oranges
1–2	grapefruit, possibly the pink-fleshed variety
1 tbsp	walnut kernels, coarsely chopped
2 tbsp	mayonnaise
2 tbsp	yoghurt or sour cream
	sandthorn juice
	Tabasco
	salt

Preparation   Wash the fruit and peel. Cut out the orange and grapefruit segments with a sharp knife, and place in a bowl. Cut the pears into pieces and mix in. Mix the mayonnaise with the yoghurt or sour cream and season to piquancy with salt, a little grated orange peel, Tabasco and sandthorn juice. Mix the fruit with this, sprinkle with the nuts, and serve in glass bowls.

Hors d'oeuvres

Danish salad

Preparation time   20 minutes

Ingredients   250 g (net weight)   beetroot, raw
250 g (net weight)   celeriac, raw
100 g   pickled gherkin or mustard gherkin
1 tsp   dill, finely chopped
1 tsp   tarragon, finely chopped
100 ml   herb vinegar dressing
1   egg, hard-boiled
4   lettuce leaves

Preparation   Slice the prepared vegetables into very thin strips (julienne). Sprinkle with the herb vinegar dressing and the finely chopped herbs. Arrange on the lettuce leaves and garnish with slices or wedges of egg. You can substitute cream cheese cubes for the egg.

Iceberg and melon salad

Preparation time	20 minutes	
Ingredients	1	iceberg lettuce
	2	carrots, coarsely grated
	½	melon, cubed or scooped
	150 ml	herb vinegar dressing
	1	soft goat's cheese
	8	black olives

Preparation Prepare and wash the lettuce, and shake dry. Mix with the grated carrot and the melon pieces. Pour on the salad dressing and mix well. Serve decorated with soft cheese cubes and olives.

Jacky cheese salad

Preparation time	20 minutes	
Ingredients	250 g	Tilsit cheese
	250 g	preserved pears
	150 g (net weight)	red pepper
	100 ml	salad dressing (see recipe p. 32), prepared without herbs
		salt
	1 tsp	parsley
		lettuce leaves to garnish

Preparation
Cut the cheese into small cubes, the pears into slices and the pepper into thin strips. Put in bowl and dress with salad dressing. Season with salt. Arrange on lettuce leaves and sprinkle with finely chopped parsley.

The pepper is more appetising if finely peeled.

Lettuce hearts

Light hors d'oeuvre, which can be added to

Preparation time	30 minutes	
Ingredients	1	head of lettuce, fresh and firm
	4	radishes
	2 tbsp	celeriac, cut into finest strips
	2 tbsp	carrots, cut into finest strips
	1 bunch	chives or chervil
	½ cup	cottage cheese
	100 ml	salad dressing (see recipe), spicily seasoned
	1 tbsp	lemon juice
		salt

Preparation   Remove the outer leaves from a head of lettuce. Cut the lettuce in quarters, wash and shake well until dry. Cut the radishes into decorative shapes and place in a little cold water so that they expand. Marinate the strips of carrot and celeriac with salt and lemon juice. Chop the chives finely. Arrange the lettuce quarters on plates, spread the vegetable strips over them and sprinkle on the dressing. Use two teaspoons to form small balls from the cottage cheese, and place next to the lettuce. Garnish with the radishes and serve sprinkled with chives.

This dish can be extended as you like by adding olives, filled eggs or savoury snacks.

Hors d'oeuvres

Madras chicory salad

Preparation   30 minutes
time

Ingredients   300 g   chicory (Belgian, Brussels)
                 1   blood orange
                 1   apple (Boskoop is very good)
                 1   banana
                 1 tbsp   almonds
                 100 ml   salad dressing (see recipe p. 32), without herbs
                 1 tsp   curry powder, mild
                 2 tbsp   whipped cream
                                         salt

Preparation   Wash the chicory and slice into 1 cm strips. Peel the orange with a knife
                 so that the white skin is also removed. Divide into 6 portions and cut
                 these into slices too. Mix the salad dressing with the curry powder and
                 the whipped cream, and dress the salad with this. Sprinkle with the
                 roasted almonds before serving.

Marinaded pepper

Preparation time	approx. 1 hour + marinading time

Ingredients	2–3	peppers, red
	2 tbsp	lemon juice
	1 clove	garlic, finely chopped
	1 tsp	parsley, finely chopped
		salt
	1 tbsp	olive oil

Preparation
Place the washed peppers on a baking tray in the oven and bake, turning once or twice, until the skin gets black spots. Remove and leave to cool, covered in a damp cloth. Peel and remove the inner compartments and seeds. Cut into bite-sized pieces and arrange on a platter. Mix a marinade of lemon juice, salt, parsley and garlic, and pour this over the peppers. Allow to marinade for several hours under cover, then sprinkle on olive oil and serve.

Hors d'oeuvres

Marinaded goat's cheese

A Ticino classic

Preparation time	15 minutes + marinading time	
Ingredients	2	soft goat's cheeses (formaggini), can also be made of cow's or sheep's milk
	2 tbsp	olive oil, best quality
	1 tsp	vinegar (cider vinegar or wine vinegar)
	1 tbsp	herbs, basil, thyme, parsley, etc.
	1 clove	garlic, finely chopped
	1 dash	Tabasco or 1 chilli pepper
	1	head of lettuce
	2 tbsp	salad dressing (see recipe)
	8	olives, black or green depending on taste

Preparation   Quarter the goat's cheeses. Mix a marinade from oil, vinegar, herbs, garlic and Tabasco and pour on the cheese quarters. Allow to marinade for at least 1 hour. Arrange lettuce leaves on a plate and sprinkle on a little salad dressing. Place the cheese quarters on these and decorate with the olives. Serve with bread or puff pastry fleurons.

Marinaded vegetables (vegetables in spice marinade)

Always a delight

Preparation time   approx. 1 hour + marinading time

Ingredients

1	bouquet garni
1	chilli pepper
1	clove
1 slice	lemon peel, thinly peeled
200 ml	water
100 ml	kvass (bread drink)
1 tsp	ginger, sliced
1 clove	garlic with peel, lightly squeezed
100 ml	olive oil
	soya sauce
	lemon juice
	salt
600–800 g	seasonal vegetables

Preparation   Wash and prepare various vegetables (carrots, asparagus, celery, etc., depending on seasonal availability) and slice them into pieces as preferred. Place the ingredients from the bouquet garni down to and including the garlic into a pot, bring to the boil, cover, turn off heat and allow to draw for about 10 minutes. Strain, add the olive oil and season strongly with soya sauce, lemon juice and salt. Keep warm. Steam or boil the vegetables in salt water until just soft, and add to the hot marinade. Cover and allow to absorb for several hours or overnight.

Hors d'oeuvres

Melon cocktail

As lovely as summer

Preparation time	30 minutes

Ingredients		
2		melons, 1 'Charantais' and 1 canteloupe or 'Honeydew' melon
1 small		head of lettuce
2–3 tbsp		mayonnaise
2–3 tbsp		salad dressing (see recipe p. 32)
100 g		cottage cheese
1 tbsp		redcurrants
1 sprig		lemon balm

Preparation Wash and halve the melons and remove seeds. Use a potato gouge to cut out melon balls, and put these in a bowl. Put in a cool place. Wash the head of lettuce, take off the leaves and dry well. Mix the mayonnaise with the salad dressing, season spicily (Tabasco, grated ginger) and pour on the melon balls. Place lettuce leaves on plates and arrange the melon balls on these. Put the cottage cheese in a fine sieve, wash under running water and allow to drain well. Spread over the melon and decorate with the lemon balm and the redcurrants.

You can use the melon flesh remaining in the skins to make a refreshing smoothie with a little milk and lemon ice or sugar.

Spicy aubergines

Hors d'oeuvre

Preparation time	30 minutes (+ several hours waiting time)

Ingredients

1–2	aubergines
1 clove	garlic
1	chilli pepper
1 sprig	rosemary
1 tbsp	vinegar
	sugar
	salt
	olive oil

Preparation

Cut the washed aubergines diagonally into 1 cm slices. Lightly salt and allow to stand for 10 minutes. Dry the aubergines on kitchen paper. Heat a little olive oil in a frying pan, and fry the aubergines in this on both sides until they are cooked. Remove them and place on a plate. Finely chop the garlic, chilli and rosemary. Gently heat two tbsp of olive oil and sauté the herbs in this. Pour on 2 tbsp of vinegar, season with a pinch of sugar and salt, and distribute this amongst the aubergines. Cover in foil and allow to marinade for several hours. Serve sprinkled with freshly chopped, flat-leaf parsley.

Lightly salted yoghurt with garlic goes very well with this.

Vegetable carpaccio

Guaranteed BSE-free!

Preparation time	30 minutes

Ingredients		
	600 g (net weight)	vegetables: kohlrabi, carrots, cucumber, radishes, etc.
	100 ml	olive oil
	1–2 tbsp	lemon juice
		Parmesan cheese as desired
	1 tsp	chives or other herbs
		herb salt

Preparation   Slice the prepared vegetables with a sharp knife or a mandolin slicer into thin strips, and arrange on a platter or individual plates. Sprinkle with a little olive oil and lemon juice, salt lightly and grate on fine slivers of Parmesan. Sprinkle with chives and serve.

Vigneron chicory salad

Preparation time	20 minutes

Ingredients	1–2	chicory (Belgian, Brussels)
	approx. 150 g	radicchio, red
	100 g	Tilsit cheese
	100 g	soft goat's cheese (formaggino)
	100 g	grapes, 'Chasselas', 'Muscat de Hambourg'
	100 ml	salad dressing (see recipe p. 32)
	2 tbsp	croutons
	½ bunch	parsley, if possible the flat-leaf variety

Preparation	Wash the lettuce, shake dry and cut into strips. Cube the cheeses into 1 cm pieces. Wash the grapes and dry. Put all ingredients into a bowl and mix with dressing. Serve sprinkled with warm croutons.

Waldorf salad

A classic

<table>
<tr><td>Preparation
time</td><td colspan="2">30 minutes</td></tr>
<tr><td>Ingredients</td><td>600 g (net weight)
200 g (net weight)
100 ml
2 tbsp</td><td>celeriac
apples, Reinette (similar to Russet) are very good
salad dressing (see recipe p. 32) without herbs
yoghurt
lemon juice
salt</td></tr>
<tr><td></td><td>50 g
4</td><td>pineapple, cut into pieces
walnut kernels
lettuce leaves to arrange on plate</td></tr>
<tr><td>Preparation</td><td colspan="2">Mix together the salad dressing and the yoghurt. Grate the celeriac and the apple into the dressing and blend in immediately. Season with salt and lemon juice. Arrange lettuce leaves in a bowl or on plates and place the salad on these. Garnish with the walnut kernels and pineapple pieces.</td></tr>
</table>

Basil
Ocimum basilicum

Basil is cold. But a man who has the palsy upon his tongue, so that he cannot speak, let him place basil under his tongue and he will recover the power of speech. But also he who has strong fever, either three-day or four-day fever, let him cook basil in wine and add honey thereto, and let him sieve this, and drink it often before breaking his fast and after the evening repast, and the fever in him will be assuaged.

Hildegard of Bingen

Cabbage salad

Preparation   20 minutes
time

Ingredients   600 g   white cabbage
                1   onion
                2 tbsp   cider vinegar
                4 tbsp   olive oil
                1 pinch   salt
                ½ tsp   caraway, roasted and chopped
                1 tbsp   diced peppers, red and green

Preparation   Slice the prepared cabbage into fine strips. Make a salad dressing by
                stirring together the vinegar, oil, onion and salt, and dress the salad with
                this. Mix in the caraway and sprinkle with the diced peppers.

Salads

Italian salad

Preparation   30 minutes + vegetable cooking time
time

Ingredients   400 g   potatoes, boiled in their skins
                150 g   celeriac, boiled
                150 g   beetroot, boiled
                2   apples, sour type
                1   pickled gherkin
                1   egg, hard-boiled
                1 tbsp   capers
                1 tbsp   vinegar (cider vinegar)
                2 tbsp   olive oil
                100 ml   salad dressing (see recipe p. 32)
                1 small   onion
                1 tbsp   chives or parsley
                                         salt, herb salt as desired
                                         lettuce leaves

Preparation   Peel the potatoes and while still warm cut them into 1 cm cubes. Likewise
                cube the beetroot, the celeriac, the quartered apples, the pickled gherkin
                and the hard-boiled egg. Roughly chop the capers or, if they are small,
                leave them whole. Finely chop the onions and mix with the vinegar. Add
                the olive oil and the salad dressing and mix well. Pour over the salad
                ingredients and mix well. Leave the salad to draw for 10 minutes, and
                season with salt and a little Tabasco if desired. Where needed, moisten
                with a little vegetable stock. Arrange on lettuce leaves and serve
                sprinkled with chives or parsley.

Lorette salad

Preparation time	30 minutes + vegetable cooking time	
Ingredients	500 g	beetroot, boiled and peeled
	500 g	celeriac, peeled and boiled
	200 g	lamb's lettuce
	200 ml	herb vinegar dressing with lots of dill and tarragon
	2	eggs, hard-boiled and peeled
Preparation	Cut the beetroot and celeriac into strips and dress separately with one portion each of the herb vinegar dressing. Arrange like bouquet. Prepare and wash the lamb's lettuce and shake dry. Shortly before serving also dress with the herb vinegar dressing and place with the other salad ingredients. Garnish with the eggs and serve with bread and butter.	

Potato, celeriac and beetroot salad

Preparation   20 minutes + vegetable cooking time
time

Ingredients   400 g   potatoes, boiled
               400 g   celeriac, boiled
               400 g   beetroot, boiled
               200 ml   herb vinegar dressing
               ½ bunch   parsley, preferably flat-leaf variety

Preparation   Peel the vegetables and cut into strips. Dress separately with the herb
               vinegar dressing and arrange like bouquet. Serve sprinkled with finely
               chopped parsley.

Radish salad

Simple and good

Preparation time	30 minutes

Ingredients	300 g (net weight)	radish, types vary with season
		salt
	1–2 tbsp	lemon juice
	approx. 100 ml	cream
	1 bunch	chives

Preparation Grate the radish and lightly salt. After about 10 minutes, crush a little and dress with lemon juice and cream. Serve sprinkled with chives.

Variation: You can also add 1 tsp dry-roasted linseed.

Raw beetroot salad

To give you a boost

Preparation time	20 minutes

Ingredients	300 g (net weight)	beetroot
	1	apple, Reinette (similar to Russet) are very good
	1 heaped tsp	horseradish, freshly grated
		head of lettuce, for arranging on plates
	2 tbsp (60 g)	quark (curd cheese)
		lemon juice
		mustard
		caraway
		salt

Preparation	Finely grate the beetroot, apple and horseradish. Mix together the quark with the lemon juice and mustard, and season with coarsely ground caraway and salt. Dress the salad with this and arrange on lettuce leaves.

> Instead of caraway you can also use fresh dill or finely grated orange peel.

Rice salad

Countless variations

Preparation time	1 hour

Ingredients		
	200 g	wholegrain rice
	1 small	bay onion
	500 g (net weight)	seasonal vegetables
	approx. 200 ml	salad dressing (see recipe p. 32)
		parsley
	1 bunch	radishes
	2–3	cloves

Preparation   Wash the rice well and bring to the boil without lid in 400 ml water. Add the bay onion to this with 2–3 cloves inserted into it, cover and cook on a low heat for about 35 minutes. Loosen grains with a fork and allow to cool. Cut the vegetables into the desired size and, depending on type, add to the rice either raw or cooked until just soft in salted water. Dress with salad dressing and season. Arrange on plates and garnish with the radishes and parsley.

Variations: For a quick version add a glass of lactic-acid fermented vegetables to the rice. Or add curry powder and fruits, boiled eggs or lentils, etc. The possibilities are endless. The same recipe is also a good accompaniment to cooked pasta (penne, small macaroni, etc.).

Salads

Rita cheese salad

Preparation time	1 hour	
Ingredients	350 g	potatoes
	300 g (net weight)	carrots
	200 g	Emmental cheese
	2	pickled gherkins
	1 small	onion or 1 bunch chives
		marjoram
		parsley
	150 ml	salad dressing (see recipe p. 32)
		salt

Preparation   Cut the cheese into strips and marinade with 2 tbsp of the salad dressing. Boil the potatoes until soft, then peel. Peel the carrots and cook until soft. Cube the vegetables and the pickled gherkins. Finely chop the onion, parsley and marjoram. Place all ingredients in a bowl and dress with salad dressing. Season with salt and possibly add a little vegetable stock if the salad seems too dry. Arrange on lettuce leaves and serve sprinkled with parsley.

Dill
Anethum graveolens

Dill is dry, warm and moderate in nature. And in whatever way it is eaten, it renders man downcast. And raw it is not fit to be eaten, because it bears greater moisture of the earth in it than does fennel, and sometimes it draws to itself some fattiness of the earth, so that it ill becomes a man to eat it raw. But cooked it suppresses gout and so it is useful with food. Therefore he from whose nose much blood flows, let him take dill and twice so much yarrow, and let him place these herbs upon his forehead, temples and chest. And these herbs must be green because their force works chiefly in the green. But when it is winter, let him pulverize these herbs, and let him sprinkle this powder with a little wine and place it in a small bag and place it upon his forehead and chest as described. […]

Hildegard of Bingen

Quark (curd cheese)

103

Avocado quark

Preparation time	10 minutes	
Ingredients	250 g	quark
	1	avocado, fully ripe
	1–2 tsp	lemon juice
	1 tsp	parsley, finely chopped
		salt
		Tabasco or white pepper, freshly milled
	1 tsp	chives

Preparation   Stir the quark until light and fluffy. If needed add a little milk or vegetable stock. Wash and peel the avocado, and dice the flesh. Mix with the lemon juice and parsley and fold into the quark. Season with salt and Tabasco. Serve sprinkled with parsley.

Quark (curd cheese) dishes

Carrot and dill quark

Preparation   10 minutes
time

Ingredients   300 g   quark, full-fat
               1 tsp   mustard
               3 tbsp   carrots, finely grated
               1 tbsp   dill, finely chopped
               1 tbsp   chives
                              herb salt
                              milk or yoghurt

Preparation   Mix the quark with the mustard, herb salt and milk or yoghurt to a smooth consistency. Fold in the carrots and the dill. Season and serve sprinkled with chives.

               The quantity of milk depends on the consistency of the quark.

Cumberland quark

Without port in this version

Preparation time	10 minutes

Ingredients	300 g	quark
	2 tbsp	redcurrant jelly
	1	orange, peel and juice
	1 tsp	mustard
		salt
		Tabasco

Preparation Stir the orange juice and redcurrant jelly with the quark until even in consistency. Add the mustard and one teaspoon of grated orange peel. Season with salt and Tabasco.

Quark (curd cheese) dishes

Herb quark

As dip with boiled potatoes in their skins

Preparation time | 10 minutes

Ingredients
350 g	quark, full-fat or low-fat quark
2 tbsp	herbs: dill, parsley, tarragon
1 tsp	mustard
1 pinch	herb salt
1 pinch	sugar

Preparation | Wash the herbs, dry them and cut finely. Add the mustard and the herbs to the quark and stir vigorously. If necessary, thin with a little milk or vegetable stock. Season with salt and sugar.

Variation: Use only one type of herb, e.g. chives or dill. In spring you can also use wild herbs such as wild garlic, stinging nettle or watercress. A mixture of finely grated carrots and fresh dill also tastes very good.

Horseradish quark

Helps prevent colds

Preparation time	10 minutes

Ingredients	350 g	quark, full-fat
	1–2 tbsp	horseradish, freshly grated
		lemon juice
		salt
		sugar

Preparation
Stir the quark to a smooth consistency. If needed, add a little milk or vegetable stock. Fold in the horseradish and season with salt, lemon juice and a pinch of sugar.

Quark (curd cheese) dishes

Quark tartare

Preparation time	15 minutes	
Ingredients	300 g	quark
	1	egg, hard-boiled
	1 tbsp	pickled gherkin, cut into small cubes
	1 tbsp	onion, finely chopped
	1 tsp	capers
	1 tsp	parsley, finely chopped
	1 tsp	mustard
		salt
		pepper or Tabasco

Preparation	Stir the quark to a smooth consistency. Mix in the other ingredients and season with salt and pepper.

Fennel
Foeniculum vulgare

Fennel has a pleasant warmth, being neither of a dry nor cold nature. Eating it raw will not do harm. And however it be eaten, it renders a person cheerful, endowing him with pleasant warmth and good sweat, and it engenders good digestion. Its seed likewise is warm in nature, and useful for health if added to other herbs in remedies. He who daily breaks his fast with fennel or its seeds, the same will lessen the sour rheum or the putrefaction within him, and suppress the foul odour of his breath. And the same will endow his eyes with clear sight by means of the good warmth and good forces. But he who is plagued by worry and cannot sleep, if it be summer, let him cook fennel moderately, and twice so much yarrow, and after pressing out the water let him lay these warm herbs upon his temples and forehead and head, and bind a cloth over this. But let him also take green sage and sprinkle it somewhat with wine, and place it thus on his heart and around his throat, and he will sleep more easily. But if it be winter, let him cook fennel seeds and root of the yarrow and place it around his head as described, and let him place pulverized sage, somewhat moistened with wine, upon his heart and throat, and it will go better for him. [...]

Hildegard of Bingen

111

Buckwheat croquettes

Preparation   1 hour including cooking time
time

Ingredients   200 g   buckwheat
              350 ml   vegetable stock
              50 g   onion
              1 tbsp (20 g)   butter
              1   egg
              1 pinch   marjoram
              1 pinch   nutmeg
              1 tbsp   parsley, finely chopped
                                         herb salt
              olive oil   for frying

Preparation   Blanch the buckwheat in boiling water, place in a sieve and rinse in
              cold water. Drain. Chop the onions finely, and fry them in butter until
              golden brown, then add the buckwheat and briefly sauté together. Pour
              on the vegetable stock, bring to the boil, then reduce to lowest heat,
              cover and allow to cook. Loosen grains with a fork and leave to cool.
              Pass half of the mass through a mincing machine, or crush well with a
              fork. Add the egg and the spices and season with herb salt. If needed,
              bind with some fine oatflakes. Use an ice cream scoop to form small
              balls and place these in a little hot fat (butter oil or olive oil), press them
              somewhat flat and fry them on both sides until crisp and brown. Place
              on kitchen paper to remove excess oil. If desired add 1 tbsp sunflower
              seeds to the mix.

Grain dishes

112

Bulghur pilau

Very good with spicy vegetable ragouts

Preparation time	25 minutes

Ingredients		
	200 g	bulghur wheat
	400 ml	vegetable stock
	1	bouquet garni
		salt
		olive oil, as desired

Preparation Bring to the boil the well-spiced vegetable stock with the bouquet garni, stir in the bulghur and bring back to the boil. Cover and allow to cook on the lowest heat or in the oven for about 20 minutes. Loosen grains with a fork, remove the bouquet garni and arrange on plates. If desired, sprinkle with a little top-quality olive oil and serve.

As a variation, mix in 1 tbsp de-stoned, coarsely chopped olives.

Green spelt pancakes

Preparation time	1 hour	
Ingredients	200 g	green spelt groats
	50 g	onion
	20 g	butter or olive oil
	400 ml	vegetable stock
	1	egg
	50 g	breadcrumbs
		marjoram
		coriander
	1 tbsp	parsley, finely chopped
		salt

Preparation   Chop the onion finely and sauté in the butter. Add the spelt, briefly sauté together and pour on the cold vegetable stock. Bring to the boil, cover and cook on the lowest heat or in the oven at 100 °C for about 20 minutes, until soft. Place in bowl, and mix in the egg and breadcrumbs. Season with the salt and spices. Form small balls with an ice cream scoop and place these in a frying pan with a little hot fat. Press the balls flat and fry on both sides until crispy brown. Place on kitchen paper to remove excess oil. The mix can be enhanced if you like with sunflower seeds or coarsely chopped hazelnuts.

The best way to press the pancakes flat is with a pastry brush dipped in oil.

Grain dishes

Green spelt groats

Basic recipe

Preparation time	30 minutes

Ingredients		
	200 g	spelt groats (bruised grain)
	400 ml	water
	1	bay onion
		herb salt

Preparation   Bring to the boil the water with the green spelt groats and the bay onion. Cover and cook on the lowest heat or in the oven at 100 °C for about 20 minutes, until soft. Then loosen with a fork and spice as desired.

Millet burgers

Preparation
time   45 minutes

Ingredients   150 g   millet
              50 g   onion, finely chopped
              1 tbsp (20 g)   butter or olive oil
              500 ml   vegetable stock
              1   egg
              40 g   millet flakes or breadcrumbs
              1 tbsp   parsley, finely chopped
              1 tbsp   sesame
                                       herb salt
              olive oil   for frying (or butter oil)

Preparation   Wash the millet thoroughly in hot water and drain. Sauté the onion in fat,
              add the millet, briefly sauté together, pour on the vegetable stock, bring
              to the boil, cover and cook on the lowest heat for about 15 minutes,
              until soft. Loosen the grains with a fork and leave to cool a little. Add
              the onion, egg, sesame and parsley and mix well. Strongly season with
              herb salt. Use an ice cream scoop to form small balls, place these in a
              frying pan with a little hot fat, and press a little flat. Fry on both sides until
              golden brown. Place on kitchen paper to remove excess fat.

For a low-fat option, the burgers can also be
cooked in the oven

Grain dishes

116

Millet dumplings

Simple but good

Preparation time	30 minutes

Ingredients		
	130 g	millet
	400 ml	milk
	1 tbsp	olive oil
	1 tsp	fenugreek
	1 pinch	allspice
		salt
	100 ml	cream
	½ tsp	paprika powder
	1–2 tbsp	Parmesan cheese

Preparation   Put the millet in a sieve and rinse in hot water. Drain well and bring to the boil with the milk, fenugreek and olive oil. Cover and leave to cool. Fork well and season with salt and allspice. Using two spoons form dumplings and put these on a greased grill tray. Stir the cream to a smooth consistency with paprika and the Parmesan, and pour over the dumplings. Grill at around 200 °C for 15 minutes.

Millet loaf

Preparation time	40 minutes + baking time

Ingredients		
	200 g	millet
	400 ml	vegetable stock
	50 g	onions
	50 g	carrots
	50 g	celeriac
	20 g	butter
	1 pinch	thyme
	1	egg
	70 g	feta cheese, in small cubes
	20 g	Parmesan cheese, freshly grated
		herb salt
	½ bunch	parsley, finely chopped
	2 tbsp	lemon juice
	50 ml	olive oil
		salt

Preparation Briefly blanch the millet in plenty of boiling water, pour off water, rinse in cold water and drain. Dice the onions, celeriac and carrots and lightly sauté with the thyme in the butter. Add the millet. Pour on the cold vegetable stock, bring to the boil, cover and cook on lowest heat for 10 minutes, until soft. Loosen grains with a fork and leave to cool a little. Fold in the egg and the two cheeses. Season with herb salt and spread the mix 1 cm thick on a greased baking tray. Leave to cool. Bake at 200 °C for about 20 minutes. To make the sauce, stir the parsley, lemon juice and olive oil together well, and season with a little salt. Take the loaf from the oven and cut into squares while still hot. Sprinkle on a little of the dressing and arrange on a hot platter. Serve the rest of the sauce in a sauceboat as accompaniment.

Grain dishes

118

Oat-nut croquettes

Preparation
time

1 hour

Ingredients

250 g	oat grains
500 ml	water
1	bay leaf
1 sprig	thyme
1 small	onion
30 g	butter
50 g	hazel nuts, roasted, shelled and coarsely crushed
1	egg
1 tbsp	chopped herbs (parsley, lovage)
1 tbsp	oat flakes
	olive oil or clarified butter for frying

Preparation

Bring to the boil the oat grains with the bay leaf, thyme and cold water, cover and cook for about 30 minutes at a low heat, until soft. Leave to cool with lid on. Chop the onion and sauté in the butter, then mix into the oat grains with the nuts, the egg and the herbs. Stir well. Season and if necessary improve the consistency of the mix with the oat flakes. Use an ice cream scoop to place half-balls of the mix in a frying pan containing a little hot fat. Press the balls flat and fry on both sides until crispy brown. Place on kitchen paper to remove excess fat.

Low-fat option: place the half-balls on a greased oven tray, brush with a little sour cream and bake in the oven.

Orsotto

Preparation time	40 minutes + soaking time	
Ingredients	200 g	barley, soaked for 3–4 hours in a little cold water
	50 g	onions
	100 g	carrots
	100 g	zucchetti (young courgette) or celery stalks
	100 ml	kvass (bread drink) or white wine
	1 l	vegetable stock, lightly salted
	1 large knife tip (25 mg)	saffron
	50 g	Parmesan cheese, freshly grated
	40 g	butter
	½ bunch	parsley, finely chopped
	1 sprig	thyme
		salt

Preparation   Finely chop the onions. Dice the courgette and carrots. Sauté the vegetables in half the butter and pour on the kvass. Allow to boil down. Add the barley with the soaking water, pour on a little vegetable stock and bring to the boil. Add the thyme and cook on low heat, stirring occasionally, until soft. If necessary add further hot vegetable stock. Add the saffron shortly before the cooking is done. When the barley is soft, fold in the rest of the butter and the Parmesan and season with salt. Serve sprinkled with parsley.

Grain dishes

Pilau rice

Basic rice recipe

Preparation time	approx. 1 hour

Ingredients		
	1 small	onion
	60 g	butter
	250 g	wholegrain rice
	exactly 500 ml	water
	1 small sprig	thyme, if desired
	1 pinch	salt to season

Preparation — Dice the onion. Melt 40 g butter in a heavy cooking pot and sauté the onion in it. Add the washed and well-drained rice and the thyme, and pour on the cold water. Bring to the boil, cover and cook on lowest heat or in the oven at 100 °C for about 50 minutes, until soft. Add the rest of the butter and a pinch of salt, and carefully loosen grains with a fork. Cover and leave to absorb for another 5 minutes

Rice cooked in this way is suitable for making dishes such as rice timbale.

Polenta

Preparation time	approx. 1 hour	
Ingredients	50 g	onions
	1 clove	garlic
	½ tsp	sage, freshly chopped
	1 tbsp	olive oil
	800 ml	vegetable stock
	200 g	polenta
		salt

Preparation   Dice the onions and the garlic and sauté in the olive oil. Add the finely chopped sage and pour on the vegetable stock. Slowly add the polenta while cooking, stirring vigorously. Bring to the boil, cover and cook for about 1 hour until soft on the lowest heat, stirring frequently.

Grain dishes

Polenta loaf

Preparation time   45 minutes

Ingredients   800 ml   vegetable stock, possibly also a half milk and half water mix
200 g   polenta
2–3   sage leaves, finely chopped
40 g   Sbrinz cheese, freshly grated
salt

Preparation   Bring to the boil the well-seasoned vegetable stock with the sage and stir in the polenta. Bring back to the boil, lower the heat and cook for about 30 minutes until soft, stirring occasionally. Fold in the Sbrinz cheese, then rinse a cake tin in cold water and place the mix in this. Allow to cool under cover. It is best to prepare this the day before. Turn out the mix onto a chopping board and cut diagonally into approx. 1.5 cm-thick slices. Dust the slices in a little flour, brush off excess, and fry the slices in hot oil until golden brown.

Variation: Dust the slices in fresh or dried herbs, place on a buttered baking tray, cover with flakes of butter and bake au gratin in hot oven.

1–2 tbsp of de-stoned green or black olives mixed into the still warm loaf makes for an interesting variation.

Polenta roulade

Not so simple, but worth the effort

Preparation time	40 minutes + baking time

Ingredients		
	300 g	polenta, not too coarsely ground
	1 l	vegetable stock
	250 g	ricotta, quark or cottage cheese
	1	egg
	1 tbsp (20 g)	Parmesan cheese
	20–30 g	breadcrumbs, depending on solidity of ricotta
	2 tbsp	pinenuts, dry-roasted
		herb salt to season
	1 bunch	parsley or a handful of spinach leaves, briefly blanched
		butter

Preparation   Stir the polenta into the boiling vegetable stock and cook for about 30 minutes on a low heat until soft, stirring occasionally. Prepare the filling of ricotta, egg, cheese, breadcrumbs and pinenuts, and season with herb salt. Moisten a clean tea towel in cold water, and spread the hot polenta on this to form a 1 cm thick, rectangular loaf. Spread the filling on the narrower length in a sausage-shape, sprinkle the remaining surface with finely chopped parsley or spinach, and form into a roll with the help of the cloth. Place on a buttered baking tray and heat again in the oven. Make sage butter by heating up butter with 1 tbsp finely chopped sage, pour on and serve.

Alternatively, leave to cool rolled in cloth, unpack and cut into 3 cm thick slices and place on a buttered baking tray. Sprinkle with butter and heat in the oven. The roulade is especially tasty if one substitutes Gorgonzola for some of the ricotta.

Grain dishes

124

Rice (dry rice)

Starting point for many rice creations

Preparation time	1 hour, 30 minutes

Ingredients		
250 g	wholegrain rice, long-grain, medium long-grain or basmati
1.25 l	water
1	bouquet garni
20 g	butter, melted
1 pinch	salt

Preparation

Thoroughly wash rice, place in the cold water and bring to the boil with the bouquet garni. Reduce the heat, cover and cook the rice for about 50 minutes until soft. Drain in a sieve and keep the cooking water. Rinse the rice in hot water, allow to drain and place in a butter-greased baking dish. Salt, cover with a cloth and lid, and place for a further 20–30 minutes in a warm oven at 80 °C. Pour the melted butter over the rice and loosen grains with a fork. The cooking water is a good basis for cream soups.

The cloth absorbs any remaining moisture, making the rice nice and loose. Millet can be prepared in the same way, but then cooking time is only 10–12 minutes.

Spinach rice

Preparation time   50 minutes

Ingredients

250 g	wholegrain rice
400 g	spinach
2 cloves	garlic
1	chilli pepper
2 tbsp	olive oil
½ bunch	dill, finely chopped
150 g	feta cheese, cut into small cubes
	salt

Preparation   Wash the rice well and leave to drain. Place in 400 ml of lightly salted, cold water in a well-sealed pot, bring to the boil and cook covered, on lowest heat, until soft, about 35–40 minutes. Place the washed spinach in a frying pan on high heat and wilt it. Take out and leave to drain. Chop coarsely. Finely chop the garlic and the chilli pepper and sauté in the olive oil. Add the rice and the spinach, mix quickly and fold in the dill and the feta cheese. Season with salt and serve immediately.

Grain dishes

Vegetable risotto

Always tasty

Preparation time	approx. 1 hour	
Ingredients	250 g	wholegrain rice
	50 g	onion, finely chopped
	1 clove	garlic, finely chopped
	1 tbsp	olive oil
	250 g (net weight)	vegetables according to season: carrots, celery, kohlrabi
	approx. 1.5 l	vegetable stock with a little salt
	1 tbsp	herbs: thyme, rosemary, sage, parsley …
	2 tbsp	Parmesan cheese, freshly grated
		salt
		olive oil as condiment

Preparation Sauté the onions and garlic in the olive oil. Add the washed, well-drained rice and the vegetables cut into cubes or strips, and pour on half the vegetable stock. Bring to the boil slowly and cook until soft on a low heat, stirring occasionally. If needed, add further boiling vegetable stock. Shortly before cooking is finished, fold in the herbs. Finally add Parmesan, and season with salt and olive oil. Serve with freshly grated Parmesan.

Savoury
Satureja montana

Savoury is more warm than cold. But someone plagued with gout so that his limbs do continually move, let him pulverize savoury and to this powder let him add a little caraway powder and a little more sage powder, and let him mix these powders together in spiced honey, and let him drink this often after eating, and it will go better with him.

Hildegard of Bingen

Cabbage roulade

A good hide-away for all sorts of things

Preparation time	40 minutes + cooking time	

Ingredients	8 leaves	white or Savoy cabbage
	1 batch	green spelt groats (bruised, see recipe p. 115)
	50 g	onions
	20 g	butter
	1 tbsp	sunflower seeds
	1	egg
	1 tbsp	parsley
	1 tsp	marjoram
		herb salt
		vegetable stock
	1 tsp	caraway

Preparation   Cut the stump/stem out of a medium-size white or Savoy cabbage and place the cabbage in boiling water for 3–5 minutes. Cool in cold water and remove eight leaves. Use a sharp knife to cut the midrib of each leaf flat so that it can be rolled better. Finely chop half of the remaining cabbage and sauté in a little butter and water until soft. Sauté the finely chopped onion in the butter, add the parsley and marjoram and briefly sauté together. Add this, with the egg and the sunflower seeds, to the green spelt groats, mix well and season with herb salt. Distribute the filling to the leaves and form roulades. Place the sautéed cabbage in a suitable stewing pot, place the roulades on top, sprinkle a little caraway around them, and place in the oven at high top heat (broiling). As soon as the roulades get brown spots, pour on vegetable stock to the top of the pot, cover and allow to cook at reduced heat for 30–40 minutes. White cabbage takes longer than Savoy. Take out the roulades and arrange on a pre-warmed platter. Boil up the contents of the pot, season and place around the roulades.

Add a little peppermint to the cooking water for all cabbage types. This gives it a better taste and makes it more digestible.

Main dishes

Cheese spätzli (noodles)

A Swabian classic accompanied by cucumber

Preparation time	30 minutes	
Ingredients	1 batch	spätzli (see recipe p. 145)
	150 g	onions
	1 sprig	sage
	1	bay leaf
	100 g	red pepper, not in original recipe
	20 g	butter
	1 bunch	chives, cut into fine reels
	100 ml	vegetable stock
	50 g	Sbrinz cheese, freshly grated

Preparation | Peel the onions and cut into fine rings. Chop the sage and the pepper into fine strips and roast with the onions and bay leaf in the butter until golden brown. Then remove the bay leaf. Mix the spätzli with half of the cheese and place in a buttered gratin dish. Spread the onion mixture over them, and sprinkle on the rest of the cheese. Put on flakes of butter and pour on the vegetable stock. Bake au gratin in a pre-heated oven until golden brown. Serve sprinkled with the chives.

Ermione pancakes

A recipe from Tuscany

Preparation time	20 minutes + 15 minutes baking time

Ingredients	1 batch	pancakes (see p. 136)
	500 g	spinach
	250 g	quark (curd cheese)
	1 sprig	basil
		pepper or chilli pepper
		salt
	100 g	Parmesan cheese, freshly grated
	100 ml	cream

Preparation   Place the washed spinach in a pot and wilt quickly on high heat. Take out, drain and chop finely. Finely chop the basil leaves and add to the spinach with the quark. Mix well and season with pepper and salt. Sprinkle the pancakes with a portion of the Parmesan and spread the spinach mix on top. Roll up and place in buttered baking tray. Sprinkle with the rest of the Parmesan, pour on the cream and bake in oven at 200 °C for about 15 minutes.

Main dishes

Fennel casserole

Ingredients   750 g   fennel
               100 g   leeks
               50 g   carrots
               50 g   celeriac
               1   bay leaf
               1 sprig   thyme
               1   chilli pepper, if desired
               2   eggs
               200 ml   vegetable stock
               100 ml   cream
                                  olive oil
               1 tbsp   Parmesan cheese
                                  coriander seeds, freshly milled
               2 stalks   parsley, finely chopped

Preparation   Prepare the fennel, and cook in plenty of salted water until just soft. Cut
               the celeriac, leeks and carrots into fine strips and sauté with the bay leaf,
               thyme and finely chopped chilli pepper in a little olive oil. Put half of
               this on the bottom of a gratin mould, place the fennel on top of this and
               spread on the rest of the vegetables. Mill the coriander over this. Whisk
               together the eggs, vegetable stock, cream and Parmesan, and season
               with salt. Pour over the vegetables and bake at 190 °C for 35 minutes.
               Serve sprinkled with parsley.

Fritata

The pleasure of cold meets warm

Preparation time	30 minutes

Ingredients		
	50 g	onions
	400 g	zucchini
	½ dl	olive oil
	½ tsp	oregano
		salt
		Tabasco
	6	eggs

Preparation: Finely chop the onions. Cut the zucchini into fine slices. Heat 2 tbsp olive oil in a frying pan and sauté the onions in this for 3–4 minutes. Leave to cool a little. Beat together the eggs with a little salt in a bowl, add the zucchini, mix and season with the spices and salt. Heat the rest of the oil in a frying pan, add the egg and vegetable mix and place the pan without lid in a pre-heated oven at 200 °C. Bake until the mixture is solid (10–15 minutes). Slide out onto a pre-warmed platter and serve sprinkled with chopped parsley. For this dish a sturdy iron frying pan is best. Otherwise, good results can also be obtained with just a non-stick pan.

> In spring you can substitute stinging nettles or wild hops for the zucchini.

Main dishes

Lentil burgers

A vegetarian hamburger

Preparation time	1 hour + soaking time + frying time	
Ingredients	180 g	lentils, brown
	½ tsp	turmeric
	100 g	bread, dry
	50 g	onions, finely chopped
	20 g	butter or olive oil
	1 clove	garlic, finely chopped
	1	chilli pepper, finely chopped
	50 g	celeriac, grated
	1 tbsp	parsley, chopped
	1–2	eggs
	1 tsp	savoury, fresh or dried
	1 tsp	mustard
		herb salt
		butter oil, clarified, for frying

Preparation Soak the washed lentils for several hours or overnight, pour off the soaking water, just cover with fresh water and cook with the turmeric until soft. Pour off the water and pass through a vegetable mincer. Soften the bread in hot water, squeeze out excess water and pass through sieve into the lentils. Sauté the onions in the butter, add celery, garlic, chilli pepper and parsley, and sauté together. Add to the lentils. Then also add the eggs and mix all well together. Season strongly with the herb salt and spices. If necessary, add some breadcrumbs. Using an ice cream scoop, form small balls of the mixture and place them in a pan with a little hot butter oil, press a little flat and fry on both sides until brown. Place on kitchen paper to remove excess fat. Serve with mixed salad or a vegetable platter.

Tip: Five-spice gives the dish an exotic flavour.

Five-spice (Panch Poron) is a mixture of equal parts of: fennel seeds, black cumin, fenugreek, cumin and black mustard seeds. If you would prefer not to mix this up yourself you can buy it ready-made from Asian food shops.

Pancakes

Preparation time   20 minutes + 20 minutes standing time

Ingredients		
100 g	bread flour (wholemeal)	
250 ml	milk	
2	eggs	
	salt	
1 pinch	nutmeg or lemon peel for sweet dishes	

Preparation   Whisk the ingredients vigorously together and leave to stand for 20 minutes. Bake thin pancakes in a suitable frying pan with a little fat.

Main dishes

Potato gnocchi

Preparation time	1 hour	
Ingredients	600 g	potatoes, boiled the day before in their skins
	120 g	flour
	1	egg
		nutmeg, freshly grated
		marjoram
		salt
	40 g	butter
	1 tsp	sage, finely chopped
	2 tbsp	Parmesan cheese, freshly grated

Preparation   Peel the potatoes and grate finely. Add the flour, egg and spices. Mix well and season with salt. Form nut-sized balls and roll these under a fork to give them the typical strip-pattern. Poach them for 5 minutes in salty water, place on a pre-warmed platter and sprinkle the Parmesan over them. Heat the butter with the sage and pour this foaming hot over the gnocchi. Serve immediately.

Variation: After cooling the gnocchi can be fried in butter.

Quark and semolina balls

A sweet-and-salty delight

Preparation   10 minutes + standing time
time

Ingredients	500 g	quark, low-fat
	1	egg
	20 g	flour
	20 g	semolina (durum wheat)
	50 g	breadcrumbs
		salt
	1 tsp	lemon peel, finely grated, for sweet dishes
	½ bunch	parsley or marjoram

Preparation   Mix all ingredients together and leave to stand for 30 minutes. Using an ice cream scoop, form balls of the mix and place in simmering salted water. After the balls rise to the surface, leave to cook for about 20 minutes. Take out the balls, spread with melted butter and serve.

Quark pancakes

Preparation time

30 minutes

Ingredients

60 g	butter
300 g	ricotta, cottage cheese or dry quark
2	eggs
approx. 70 g	breadcrumbs, depending on quark consistency
1 tbsp	parsley, finely chopped
	salt, to season
1–2 tbsp	pinenuts, dry-roasted, or chopped walnuts, sesame, etc.

Preparation   Whisk the butter until light and frothy, add the ricotta, eggs and bread-crumbs, and season with salt. Fold in the roasted pinenuts. Using an ice cream scoop, place small balls of the mix into a frying pan with a little fat, press gently flat and fry on both sides until golden brown.

Ricotta gnocchi

Preparation time	40 minutes	

Ingredients	400 g	ricotta or cottage cheese
	2	eggs
	100 g	semi-white flour (strong bread flour)
	80 g	Parmesan cheese or Sbrinz
	½ bunch	parsley or basil, dill, sage, etc.
		herb salt
	1 tbsp	butter
	1 tsp	sage leaves

Preparation	Mix well together the ricotta, eggs, flour and parsley in a bowl, and season with herb salt. Leave to stand for 10 minutes. Using a piping bag with a large, flat spout, or 2 spoons, form 2 cm balls and place in simmering, salted water. After they rise to the surface leave to cook for a further 3–4 minutes. Place on a pre-warmed platter. Heat the butter together with the sage leaves cut into fine strips, and pour foaming hot over the gnocchi. Serve immediately. Separately serve freshly grated Parmesan cheese as accompaniment.

You can also cover the gnocchi in a little Parmesan and butter flakes, and lightly bake au gratin in the oven.

Main dishes

140

Roman gnocchi

Preparation time	25 minutes + baking time	
Ingredients	600 ml	milk
	25 g	butter
	125 g	semolina (durum wheat)
		salt
		nutmeg
	1	egg yolk
	50 g	Parmesan cheese, freshly grated
		butter for greasing tin

Preparation   Bring to the boil the milk with the butter, salt and nutmeg. While stirring, pour in the semolina, and cook for 10–15 minutes on low heat while continuing to stir. Remove from heat and stir half the cheese and the egg yolk into the mixture. Using a pastry scraper spread this 2 cm thick on a tray rinsed in cold water, and leave to cool. After cooling turn out onto the work surface. Using a round pastry mould (5 cm) cut out circles or half-moon shaped pieces and arrange these like roof tiles on a buttered gratin dish. Sprinkle with the rest of the Parmesan cheese. Distribute flakes of butter over this and bake au gratin at 200 °C until golden brown.

Rösti

Always tasty

Preparation time	30 minutes

Ingredients	800 g	potato, cooked in skins on previous day
	50 g	butter
		salt

Preparation — Peel the cooked potatoes and grate. Heat half the butter in a frying pan and sauté the potatoes, turning occasionally and salting lightly. Form round flat-cakes from this and continue to fry until the underside is golden brown. Turn with the help of a lid. Put the rest of the butter in the pan and fry the rösti on the other side until brown.

Main dishes

Sauerkraut strudel

Preparation
time

approx. 2 hours

Ingredients

250 g	semi-white flour, plain
100 ml	water, lukewarm
1 tbsp (20 ml)	sunflower oil
1 small	egg
1 tsp (10 ml)	vinegar (cider vinegar)
1 pinch	salt
500 g	sauerkraut, cooked and cooled
20 g	butter
50 g	breadcrumbs
100 ml	sour cream
1 tsp	dill, fresh or dried
	herb salt

Preparation

Make a dough from the flour, water, oil, egg, vinegar and salt, and knead this until it shines and is no longer sticky. The consistency should be soft and elastic. Cover and leave in a warm place for at least one hour. Place the sauerkraut to drain in a sieve. Heat the butter and roast the breadcrumbs in this until golden brown. Stir together the sour cream with the dill, and season with herb salt. Roll out the strudel dough with a little flour, place on clean tea towel and pull with the hands as thinly as possible into a square. Put the breadcrumbs on a third of this surface, and the sauerkraut on top. Pour on the sour cream and use the tea towel to roll up loosely. Place on baking tray greased with melted butter and bake for about 30 minutes at 200 °C.

The strudel also tastes very good with spinach, leeks, squash or a mixture of these. Important: the filling must be strongly seasoned.

Semolina gnocchi

Preparation time	40 minutes	
Ingredients	600 ml	milk or water
	60 g	butter
	1 pinch	salt
	1 pinch	nutmeg, freshly grated
	200 g	semolina (durum wheat), very good with wholegrain wheat or spelt semolina
	3	eggs
	1 tbsp	parsley, finely chopped
	20 g	butter
	1 tbsp	sage leaves, cut into strips

Preparation   Bring to the boil the milk with the butter, salt and nutmeg, and quickly stir in the semolina. Vigorously stir until the mix comes free of the pan and sticks together. Place in bowl, leave to cool a little and work in one egg after another. Finally fold in the parsley. Season. With a piping bag or 2 spoons, form nut-size balls and place these in gently simmering water. After the gnocchi rise to the surface leave for three minutes to cook on low heat (below simmering point). Place on a buttered platter with a skimmer spoon and leave in a warm place until all are ready. Whip up the sage strips with the melted butter until light and fluffy and pour over the gnocchi. Serve with freshly grated Parmesan.

> If one separates the eggs and first folds the yolk into the mixture and then the egg white whipped stiff, the mix can be placed in a greased mould and baked as casserole in the oven.

Main dishes

144

Spätzli (noodles)

Swabian favourite

Preparation time	50 minutes (including standing time)

Ingredients		
	250 g	bread flour (wholemeal flour) or 150 g bread flour plus
	100 g	durum wheatmeal
	2	eggs
	150–200 ml	water, lukewarm
		salt to taste
	1 pinch	nutmeg, freshly grated

Preparation   Mix all ingredients together well and beat strongly (kitchen mixer). Leave covered for 20 minutes. Use a dedicated spätzli maker to form noodles, and place these in simmering, salted water, then bring to the boil. As soon as the spätzli rise to the surface, take them out with a skimming spoon, place on a platter, cover and keep warm. Repeat the process until the dough has been used up. To serve, either warm the spätzli in some melted butter or heat in the cooking water and lightly butter after draining.

As variation, add some blanched, finely chopped nettle tips to the dough.

Spinach cake

Preparation time	1 hour	
Ingredients	8	pancakes (20 cm diameter, see basic pancake recipe p. 136)
	800 g	spinach
	50 g	shallots
	1 clove	garlic
	1	chilli pepper
	20 g	butter
	150 g	mozzarella
		salt
		pepper

Preparation   Finely chop the shallots, garlic and chilli pepper and sauté in the butter. Wash the spinach, drain and place in a preheated pot. Shrink down on high heat. Remove and drain. Chop coarsely and add to the shallot mixture. Mix well and season with salt, pepper and nutmeg. Place a pancake on a greased gratin dish and place a portion of the spinach on it. Cover with the next pancake and again place some spinach on this. Continue until all pancakes are included, finishing with a pancake on top. Bake this 'cake' for 20 minutes at 180 °C. Remove and 'ice' with the mozzarella cut into slices. Put back in the oven until the cheese has melted. A carrot ragout goes very well with this.

Main dishes

Spinach dumplings

Preparation time	45 minutes	
Ingredients	60 g	onions, finely chopped
	1 clove	garlic, finely chopped
	1	chilli pepper, de-seeded if desired, finely chopped
	1 tbsp (20 g)	sunflower seeds
	120 g	grain groats (preferably oats, green spelt or barley), already cooked until soft
	500 g (net weight)	spinach
	80 g	bread (dry)
	2	eggs
		marjoram or dill
		Tabasco
		salt
		olive oil or butter oil

Preparation   Sauté the onion in a little fat. After 5 minutes add the garlic and chilli pepper and briefly sauté together. Soften the bread in a little hot water, squeeze out excess water and pass through vegetable mincer. Place the washed, still wet spinach in a pot and shrink down on high heat. Take out and drain, then chop not too finely with a knife. Mix together well the onion, bread, spinach, sunflower seeds, grain and eggs, and season with the salt and spices. If the mix is too moist, add some breadcrumbs. With two spoons or an ice cream scoop form the dumplings and fry on both sides in the frying pan in olive oil or butter oil. Place on kitchen paper to remove excess fat.

Spinach pudding

A classic

Preparation time	30 minutes + 75 minutes cooking time

Ingredients		
	500 g	spinach, cooked, drained then weighed
	1 tbsp (20 g)	butter
	1	egg yolk
	40 g	breadcrumbs
	100 ml	cream
		nutmeg, freshly grated
		marjoram
		salt
	1	egg white
		butter, to grease tin
		breadcrumbs for the tin

Preparation	Pass the spinach through a fine sieve. Stir the soft butter and the egg yolk until light and fluffy. Fold in the spinach, breadcrumbs and cream, and strongly season with salt and spices. Whip the egg white plus a pinch of salt until stiff, and carefully fold into the mixture. Generously grease a (750 ml) pudding mould with butter and sprinkle with breadcrumbs. Fill it with the mixture and close lid. Cook in pot of simmering water for 75 minutes. Before turning out leave to stand for 5 minutes. Serve with a herb sauce.

Main dishes

Swiss chard bake

The best way to enjoy Swiss chard

Preparation time	25 minutes + baking time

Ingredients		
	600 g	Swiss chard, just the green leaves
	2	eggs
	50 g	croutons, strongly flavoured with garlic
	100 ml	cream
	2 tbsp	sunflower seeds, dry-roasted
	100 g	feta cheese
	1 pinch	marjoram
	1 pinch	nutmeg
		salt
		Tabasco if desired

Preparation   Boil the washed chard leaves in plenty of salted water until soft, drain and chop coarsely. Mix with the other ingredients and season strongly with the spices and salt. Grease a suitable cake tin with butter and line with baking paper. Fill it with the mixture and place on a high-sided baking tray. Put a little hot water in the baking tray, and cook in the oven for 40–50 minutes at 200 °C (skewer test). Before turning out, leave to stand for 5 minutes. Turn out onto a breadboard and cut into approx. 2 cm slices with a sharp knife.

Vegetable skewers

A different kind of kebab

Preparation time	40 minutes + 15 minutes baking time (+ marinading time)

Ingredients	32	pieces of cubed vegetable for 4 kebabs
	500 ml	vegetable stock
	8 leaves	sage or basil
	1 clove	garlic, finely squeezed
	2 tbsp	lemon juice
	1 tbsp	olive oil
	1 tsp	herbes de Provence
		salt
	1 tsp	Parmesan cheese
	½ tsp	lemon peel, fine
	1 tbsp	breadcrumbs

Preparation Prepare various kinds of seasonal vegetable such as carrots, kohlrabi, pepper, zucchini, shallots, Brussels sprouts etc. and cut into 2–3 cm cubes. This is unnecessary for the shallots and Brussels sprouts. Cook the vegetables separately, or if it works together, in the well-spiced vegetable stock until just soft. Cool in cold water, remove and drain. Skewer on wooden kebab sticks, alternating vegetables with the sage leaves. Stir the olive oil, lemon juice, garlic and herbes de Provence vigorously together and season with salt. Spread this over the kebabs with a brush and leave to marinade for at least 1 hour, preferably overnight, in the fridge. Place on a lightly greased baking tray. Mix together Parmesan, lemon peel and breadcrumbs and sprinkle on the kebabs. Drip on a little olive oil and bake at 200 °C for about 15 minutes.

Tip: You can replace some of the vegetable cubes with a hard baking cheese (such as Halloumi).

Viennese dumplings (bread dumplings)

Preparation time	30 minutes + 20 minutes cooking time

Ingredients		
400 g	yesterday's wheat bread or rolls
approx. 250 ml	milk, hot
50 g	onions, finely chopped
40 g	butter
1 bunch	parsley, finely chopped
2–3	eggs, depending on size
1 tbsp	semi-white flour, plain
	nutmeg
	caraway
	salt

Preparation   Cut the bread into 1 cm cubes and pour the hot milk over it. Sauté the onions in the butter, and when golden brown add the parsley. Briefly sauté together and add to the softened bread. Likewise add the whisked eggs and the flour to the bread. Mix well and strongly season with freshly grated nutmeg, milled caraway and salt. Mould a test-dumpling and put in simmering water. If it does not stick together, add some more flour to the mix. Form balls and cook in simmering water for about 20 minutes after they have risen to the surface. Remove with a skimming spoon and serve.

The quantity of milk needed is very much dependent on the dryness of the bread. You can also use slightly stale white rolls. If the bread is still very moist, one should place the bread cubes in the oven briefly to dry.

Garlic
Allium sativum

Garlic has warmth to the right degree, and it grows forth from the strength of the dew; and it is quick from the beginning of the night until close to the dawn, and into daylight. For those both healthy and sick it is more wholesome to eat than leek. And it must be eaten raw, for he who would cook it would make of it so to speak spoiled wine: it would become sour, for uncooked its juice is moderate and has the right property of warmth. Nor does it harm the eyes. Nonetheless, due to its properties of warmth, it greatly excites the blood around man's eyes, but later they do become clear. But it should be eaten in moderation so that it does not excessively warm man's blood. But when the garlic is old, then its healthy and proper juice is diminished; yet when moderated again by other dishes, it regains it strength once more.

Hildegard of Bingen

Aubergine ramekin

Preparation time   25 minutes + 35 minutes baking time

Ingredients

200 g	raclette cheese
1 sprig	rosemary
1 clove	garlic
2 tbsp	herbs: parsley, oregano, thyme
½ tsp	paprika powder
2	eggs
200 ml	vegetable stock or milk
1 tbsp	olive oil
	salt
1 tbsp	parsley, finely chopped
1 tbsp	black olives, de-stoned and quartered
500 g	aubergines

Preparation   Cut the unpeeled aubergines into 1 cm thick, lengthways slices, and cook in salted water with the rosemary and garlic clove until just soft. Place in sieve to drain. Cut the cheese into thin slices and, alternating with the aubergines, arrange in roof-tile pattern on a low-sided, greased gratin dish. Finely chop the herbs, mix with the paprika, eggs, vegetable stock and olive oil, and season with salt. Pour over the aubergines, strew the olives on top, and cook in oven at 175 °C for about 35 minutes.

Also tastes good with zucchini.

Beetroot gratin

Preparation
time

40 minutes + cooking time

Ingredients	600 g	beetroots
	200 ml	sour cream
	1	egg
	1 tbsp	dill, fresh, finely chopped
	1 tsp	parsley, fresh, finely chopped
	1 tsp	horseradish, freshly grated
	1 tsp	mustard
		salt
		butter for greasing

Preparation   Boil the beetroots until soft, peel and cut into approx. 6 mm slices. Grease a gratin dish and layer the beetroot slices like roof tiles. Lightly sprinkle with salt and half the parsley. Stir the rest of the ingredients together well, season with salt and pour over the beetroot. Bake for about 20 minutes at 180–200 °C.

As a variation, you can substitute capers for the horseradish.

Buckwheat casserole

Preparation time   30 minutes + 35 minutes baking time

Ingredients

200 g	buckwheat
300 ml	milk
300 ml	water
100 g	onions
1 tbsp (20 g)	butter
1 tbsp	soya sauce
	salt to taste
	marjoram
	pepper or Tabasco
2	eggs
	butter for the dish

Preparation   Place the buckwheat in boiling water and blanch for 1 minute. Pour off water, rinse in cold water, and drain. Bring the water and milk to the boil, add the buckwheat and cook for about 20 minutes until soft. Leave to cool a little. Finely chop the onions and fry in the butter until golden yellow. Separate the eggs and add the yolks to the buckwheat. Mix and season with soya sauce, salt, marjoram and Tabasco or pepper. Whip the egg white until stiff and fold into the mix. Fill a greased casserole, dribble on a little melted butter and bake in the oven at 200 °C for about 35 minutes.

Casseroles and gratins

156

Cheese bake (ramekin)

Preparation time	20 minutes	
Ingredients	10 slices	white bread, preferably Ticino bread
	10 slices	raclette cheese or Gruyère
	3	eggs
	500 ml	milk
		salt
		nutmeg
		parsley
		paprika powder

Preparation   Arrange the bread and cheese in alternating 'tile' rows in a buttered gratin dish. Whisk together the eggs and milk, season with salt and nutmeg, and pour over the bread and cheese. Bake through in the oven at 180° C, browning au gratin at the same time, for about 30 minutes. Before serving sprinkle with paprika and chopped parsley.

Cheese bake (soufflé)

The guests can wait but not the soufflé!

Preparation time   50 minutes

Ingredients

50 g	butter
50 g	flour
300 ml	milk
100 g	Sbrinz cheese, freshly grated
2	egg yolks
	salt
	nutmeg, freshly grated
	paprika powder
2	egg whites

Preparation   Bring the milk to the boil and then turn off. Heat the butter and flour in a pot and stir well. Leave to cool a little, then add the hot milk, stirring as you do so, and bring to the boil. Stir on the heat until you get a smooth mass. Leave to cool slightly and fold in the egg yolk and the cheese. Season with nutmeg, paprika and salt. Whip the egg white until stiff and strongly work about a quarter of the quantity into the cheese mix. Loosely fold in the rest. Fill a greased casserole to a depth of three quarters, and bake on a rising temperature from 160 °C to 200 °C for 30–35 minutes. Serve immediately.

Casseroles and gratins

Chicory gratin

Preparation   45 minutes
time

Ingredients   600 g   chicory (Belgian, Brussels)
               1 tbsp   lemon juice
               2   eggs, hard-boiled
               250 ml   cream sauce (see recipe p. 21)
               2 tbsp   Sbrinz cheese, freshly grated
               1 tbsp   walnut kernels, chopped

Preparation   Make a 2–3 cm lengthwise cut in the washed and prepared chicory
               stems, and cook until just soft in salted water to which lemon juice has
               been added. Place evenly in a buttered gratin dish, cover with the sliced
               eggs and pour on the cream sauce. Sprinkle the grated cheese and the
               walnut kernels on top and dribble on a little melted butter. Bake au gratin
               in a hot oven for about 20 minutes until golden brown.

               The same recipe also tastes good with Brussels
               sprouts.

Chilean sweetcorn casserole

A dish of ancient origins

Preparation time	1 hour	
Ingredients	50 g (1 small)	onion
	1 small	red pepper
	80 g	olives, black and green, de-stoned and quartered
	1 tbsp	olive oil
	400 g	sweetcorn, fresh in the autumn, otherwise tinned
	1 tbsp (25 g)	raisins, soaked
	1 tsp	parsley, finely chopped
	2 pinches	caraway
	1 pinch	paprika powder
		salt
	1	egg, hard-boiled and roughly chopped
	100 g	sweetcorn
	2 tbsp	water
	1	egg

Preparation   Finely chop the onion, quarter the pepper and cut into fine strips. Sauté in the olive oil, and add the olive quarters, the 400 g of sweetcorn, the drained raisins, the hard-boiled egg and the spices. Mix well and season with salt. Mix the rest of the sweetcorn with the water and the egg yolk and add to the mix. Whip the egg white until stiff, and likewise fold in. Place in a greased casserole and bake for about 35 minutes in a medium oven (180 °C).

Casseroles and gratins

160

Epicurean celeriac

The name says it all

Preparation time	40 minutes

Ingredients		
	600 g	celeriac
	1 tbsp	lemon juice
	½	bay leaf
	1	clove
	½	chilli pepper
	1 tbsp (20 g)	butter
	1 tbsp (20 g)	flour
	150 ml	milk
	1	egg
	150 g	Sbrinz cheese, freshly grated
		nutmeg
		salt
	1 small	onion
	1 tbsp	butter
	2–3 leaves	sage
	1 slice	pineapple, fresh or preserved
	8	cherries, preserved
	2 stalks	parsley

Preparation   Peel the celeriac and cut into approx. 1 cm slices, to give 8 slices. Boil in salted water with lemon juice, bay leaf, clove and chilli pepper until just soft. Stir the flour in the melted butter until smooth, pour on the hot milk and bring to the boil while stirring. Cover and leave to stand for 10 minutes, then stir in the egg and the Sbrinz cheese and season with salt and nutmeg. Peel the onion and cut into thin rings. Slowly roast in the butter, together with the sage. Remove the celeriac slices from the cooking water and arrange next to each other on a greased baking tray. Use a piping bag to spread the cheese sauce on the celeriac slices, and place the onion rings on top. Cut the pineapple slice into eight and place each piece sideways into the cheese mixture. Cook au gratin in a hot oven (200 °C) until golden brown, arrange on a hot platter and garnish with parsley and the preserved cherries.

Aubergines are also very good for this recipe.

Grandmother's cheese bake

Preparation
time

40 minutes + 25 minutes in the oven

Ingredients

1 tbsp (15 g)	butter
1 tbsp (15 g)	flour
300 ml	milk
200 g	white bread (toast bread) cubed
1 small	onion, finely chopped
1 tbsp	butter
2	eggs
70 g	Sbrinz cheese
	nutmeg
	marjoram
	salt

Preparation

Prepare a béchamel sauce (see recipe p. 20) from the butter, milk and flour. In the meantime, bake the bread cubes in the oven until golden brown. Sauté the onion in the butter. Separate the egg yolk from the egg white. Mix the yolk, onion, cheese and bread with the sauce, season with the spices and salt, and fold in the whipped egg white. Fill a buttered casserole and bake at 180 °C for about 30 minutes.

Casseroles and gratins

Gratin dauphinois

A classic

Preparation time	30 minutes + 1 hour in the oven

Ingredients		
	600 g	potatoes, peeled and weighed
	80 g	Sbrinz cheese, or half Sbrinz, half Gruyère
	2 cloves	garlic
	300 ml	milk
	100 ml	cream
	1 pinch	nutmeg, freshly grated
		salt
	½	bay leaf

Preparation   Bring to the boil the milk and cream with the bay leaf, and leave to cool. Take out the bay leaf. Slice the potatoes finely or shave-grate (2 mm) and mix with 60 g grated cheese and the finely chopped garlic. Fill a buttered gratin dish. Spice the milk with nutmeg and salt and pour over the potatoes. Sprinkle the rest of the cheese on top and dribble on a little melted butter. Bake for 1 hour in the oven at 170 °C.

If desired, the potatoes can be additionally seasoned with a pinch of marjoram.

Gruyère gratin

Simple and good

Preparation time	30 minutes + 40 minutes in the oven

Ingredients		
	80 g	oatflakes, fine
	80 g	barley flakes, coarse
	250 ml	water
	120 g	Gruyère cheese, grated
	150 ml	cream
	2	eggs, separated
	1 tbsp	parsley, finely chopped
		herb salt
		butter for greasing

Preparation   Mix the flakes with the water and allow to swell for 20 minutes. Add the Gruyère, the parsley, the cream and two egg whites, and mix well. Season with herb salt. Whip the egg whites until stiff and carefully fold in. Fill a buttered casserole, dribble on a little melted butter and bake for 40 minutes at 170–180 °C.

Casseroles and gratins

Leek gratin

Tasty variation of spinach Roussillon

Preparation time	1 hour	
Ingredients	600 g (net weight)	leeks
	1 tsp	ginger, fresh, finely chopped
	1 tsp	black mustard seeds
	3 tbsp	olive oil
		vegetable stock
	100 g (3 slices)	toasting bread, wholegrain
	50 g	onions, finely chopped
	1	chilli pepper, finely chopped, de-seeded if desired
	1 clove	garlic, finely chopped
		nutmeg, finely grated
	½ bunch	parsley, finely chopped
	150 ml	cream sauce (see recipe p. 21)
	100 g	mozzarella cheese, cut into slices

Preparation   Lightly roast the ginger and mustard seeds in oil, add the washed leek that has been cut into fine strips (1 cm), and gently sauté for 30 minutes on low heat, adding a little vegetable stock. Sauté the onions in the rest of the olive oil, adding the garlic and chilli pepper after 5 minutes, and continuing to sauté for a further 5 minutes. Cut the bread into 1 cm cubes and add. Continue to fry while stirring until the bread is lightly roasted. Add with the cream sauce and the parsley to the leeks, and carefully mix together. Season with herb salt and nutmeg. Place in a greased gratin dish and bake at 200 °C for about 20 minutes. Take out and cover with the sliced mozzarella, then bake again for 5 minutes until the cheese has melted. The cheese should not change colour.

Noodles au gratin

Simple and good

Preparation time	30 minutes

Ingredients		
	250–300g	noodles, thick (uncooked weight)
	200 ml	cream sauce (see recipe p. 21)
		salt
		nutmeg, freshly grated
	50 g	Parmesan cheese, freshly grated
	1 tsp	sage, cut into strips
	1 tbsp	butter

Preparation   Cook the noodles in plenty of salted water until just soft, pour off the water and mix with the cream sauce and the sage, and season with salt and freshly grated nutmeg. Place in a buttered gratin dish, sprinkle with the Parmesan and dribble on melted butter. Cook au gratin in an oven with high top heat (200 °C).

Casseroles and gratins

Quark and potato casserole

Milder version of the gratin dauphinois

Preparation time	1 hour 20 minutes

Ingredients		
	700 g	potatoes
	80 g	Gruyère cheese, grated
	250 g	quark, full-fat
	200 ml	milk
	1	egg
	1 tbsp	parsley, finely chopped
		nutmeg, freshly grated
		salt or herb salt
		butter for greasing

Preparation Boil the potatoes, peel and slice them and place in a buttered gratin dish. Stir the other ingredients together and season strongly with salt and nutmeg. Keep back a little of the grated cheese. Pour the mix over the potatoes, sprinkle with the rest of the cheese and dribble on a little melted butter. Cook in oven at 180–200 °C for about 30 minutes, browning lightly.

Potatoes in their skins taste more aromatic if a clove and half a bay leaf are added to the cooking water.

Rice casserole

Preparation
time
   1 hour 20 minutes including boiling and baking time

Ingredients

250 g	wholegrain rice
1 small	bay onion
600 ml	water
1	egg
200 ml	milk
250 ml	vegetable stock
1 small sprig	thyme
1 small sprig	rosemary
5 stalks	parsley
	salt
	butter for greasing

Preparation   Wash and drain the rice. Bring to the boil the water with the bay onion and the rice, then cover and simmer on low heat. After 30 minutes most of the water should have been absorbed and the rice should be almost soft. Leave to cool a little. Whisk up the egg with the milk and vegetable stock. Pluck the herb leaves from their stalks, chop finely and, together with the egg mix, add to the rice. Season with salt. Place in a buttered casserole, lightly dribble with melted butter and bake at 180 °C for 35–40 minutes. You may wish to cover the dish for the first 25 minutes.

As variation, season the rice with curry powder or nuts.

Casseroles and gratins

Roussillon spinach gratin

Preparation time
1 hour including baking time

Ingredients

600 g (net weight)	spinach
3 slices	wholegrain or wheat bread
50 g (1 small)	onion
1 clove	garlic
2 tbsp (50 g)	butter or olive oil
½ tsp	marjoram
	salt
	nutmeg, freshly grated
1	chilli pepper, finely chopped (fresh or dried)
100 g	mozzarella cheese, cut into small cubes

Preparation
Place the washed and still wet spinach in a frying pan and wilt at high heat. Place in sieve to drain, then chop coarsely. Cut the bread into cubes. Finely chop the onion and the garlic and sauté with the chilli pepper in the fat, then add the bread cubes and briefly sauté together. Add three-quarters of the mix to the spinach, fold in and season with marjoram, salt and nutmeg. Fill a buttered baking tray, place the last quarter of the bread mix on the spinach and bake for about 20 minutes in a medium oven. Now sprinkle the mozzarella over the bake and re-place in oven for a further 5 minutes. The cheese should only melt and not change colour.

Sauerkraut casserole

Central European version of shepherd's pie

Preparation time	1 hour 30 minutes

Ingredients		
	500 g	potatoes, peeled and weighed
	200 ml	milk, hot
	20 g	butter
		salt
		nutmeg
	500 g	sauerkraut, cooked
	1 small	egg
	1 tbsp	butter

Preparation — Boil the potatoes until soft, pour off water and leave to dry off. Pass through a sieve and make a potato purée with milk, butter, salt and nutmeg. Place the sauerkraut in a greased casserole. Put the purée in a piping bag and cover the sauerkraut evenly with it. Melt the butter and whisk up with the egg, then brush over the purée. Bake for about 30 minutes at 180–200 °C.

Casseroles and gratins

Savoury quark casserole

Preparation time	10 minutes + 35 minutes in the oven

Ingredients	500 g	quark (curd cheese), also works well with low-fat quark
	2	eggs, separated
	50 g	semolina (durum wheat)
	100 ml	milk
	100 ml	cream
	100 g	Sbrinz cheese, freshly grated
		nutmeg, freshly grated
		salt
	1 tbsp	parsley, finely chopped

Preparation   Mix the quark, egg yolks, semolina, cream, milk, grated cheese and parsley together well. Whip the egg white, plus a pinch of salt, until stiff and fold into the quark mix. Season with salt and nutmeg and fill a greased casserole. Bake for about 35 minutes at 180–200 °C.

Squash gratin

Squash at its best

Preparation time	50 minutes including baking time	
Ingredients	50 ml	vegetable stock
	600 g (net weight)	squash
	100 g	feta cheese, cubed
	2–3 tbsp	croutons (see recipe p. 54)
	1 tbsp	pinenuts
	200 ml	sour cream
		herb salt
	1 pinch	curry powder
	1 tbsp	Parmesan cheese, freshly grated
	1 tsp	parsley, finely chopped
	4–6	black olives

Preparation
Cut the squash into 2 cm cubes and sauté in the well-spiced vegetable stock until just soft. Take out with the skimming spoon and place in a buttered baking tray. Lightly roast the pinenuts in a dry pan and add to the squash together with the croutons. Stir the sour cream with curry powder, Parmesan and parsley until smooth. Season with herb salt and pour over the squash. Spread the olives over this and briefly bake under top heat in a hot oven at 200 °C.

Casseroles and gratins

Sweetcorn casserole

Preparation time   1 hour including baking time

Ingredients
200 g	cornflour
500 ml	milk
500 ml	water
1 tbsp (20 g)	butter or olive oil
1 tbsp	pinenuts
2	eggs
1 tsp	sage, finely chopped
1 pinch	thyme
	nutmeg, freshly grated
2 tbsp	Parmesan cheese, freshly grated
	salt
	butter for greasing

Preparation   Bring to the boil the milk, butter and water, salt the mixture and stir in the cornflour. Bring back to the boil and allow to simmer on the lowest heat for 20 minutes. Lightly roast the pinenuts in a dry pan. Separate the eggs and fold the egg yolk, pinenuts, herbs and the Parmesan into the slightly cooled mix. Season with salt and nutmeg. Whip the egg white until stiff, and loosely fold in. Fill a buttered casserole dish, dribble on a little melted butter and bake for 30–35 minutes in a medium oven (200 °C).

Vegetable soufflé

Preparation   40 minutes + 35 minutes in the oven
time

Ingredients   40 g   butter
               40 g   flour
               300 ml   milk
               2   egg yolks
               30 g   Parmesan cheese
                                             nutmeg, freshly grated
                                             salt
               500 g   vegetables: fennel, carrots, celery, leek, etc.
               3   egg whites
                                             salt
                                             vegetable stock

Preparation   Make a thick béchamel sauce (see recipe p. 20) from butter, flour and
               milk, and leave to cool, stirring occasionally. Stir in the egg yolk and
               cheese and season with nutmeg and salt. Cut the vegetables into cubes
               (1.5 cm) and cook in a little vegetable stock. Drain and mix with the
               béchamel. Whip the egg white plus a pinch of salt until stiff, and care-
               fully fold into the mixture. Fill a buttered casserole (to three quarters of its
               depth) and bake at 200 °C for about 35 minutes. Serve immediately.

Casseroles and gratins

Zucchini ramekin

| Preparation time | 1 hour including baking time |

Ingredients	3 medium	zucchini
	100–150 g	raclette cheese, in thin slices
	1–2	eggs
	150 ml	vegetable stock
	1 tbsp	black olives, de-stoned and roughly chopped
	1 tbsp	parsley, finely chopped
		salt
		oregano
		pepper or Tabasco
		olive oil

Preparation
Cut the washed zucchini lengthways into approx. 6 mm slices. Blanch for a few seconds in boiling, salted water. Drain and spread to cool. Lightly grease a rectangular porcelain baking dish with olive oil and arrange the zucchini slices in this, alternating and overlapping with the cheese slices. Whisk the eggs well with the vegetable stock and the spices, pour over the zucchini and place olives on top. Dribble on a little olive oil and bake in a hot oven (180–200 °C) for about 25 minutes.

Caraway
Carum carvi

Caraway is of moderate warmth, and dry. It is good and useful and healthy to eat for a person who is vaporous, in whichever way it be eaten. But it is harmful to him who suffers with pain in the heart, because it does not wholly warm the heart, which must always be warm. For a healthy man, however, it is good to eat, for it induces in him good reason, and to him who is too warm brings milder warmth. He who is ill, however, takes injury from eating thereof, for it lets the disease flare up within him, excepting he who suffers with pain in the lung. A man who desires to eat cooked or roasted cheese, let him strew caraway thereon, so that he may not suffer pain in consequence, and then let him eat. But he who suffers with queasiness, let him take caraway, and a third as much pepper, and a quarter as much burnet, and let him pulverize the same; and let him take breadcrumbs and strew this powder amongst the breadcrumbs, and so let him make small cakes therefrom, with egg yolk and moderate water, either in the warm oven or under the warm ash, and let him eat these small cakes. But let him also eat the above-named powder sprinkled upon bread, and it will suppress in the bowels both the warm and cold fluids which cause queasiness to man.

Hildegard of Bingen

Baked fennel

Preparation time	40 minutes	
Ingredients	750 g	fennel
	75 g	Sbrinz cheese
	2 tbsp	butter
	½ tsp	coriander seeds, pounded roughly
	1 pinch	oregano

Preparation   Quarter and wash the fennel. Finely chop the delicate green fronds. Cook the fennel in salted water until just soft, drain and layer in a buttered casserole. Sprinkle on the chopped fennel greens, coriander, oregano and the cheese. Lightly dribble with butter and bake au gratin in a hot oven until golden brown.

Vegetables

Caraway potatoes

Preparation time	15 minutes + approx. 20 minutes baking

Ingredients		
	600 g	potatoes, medium size
	2 tbsp	caraway
	1 tbsp	olive oil
		salt

Preparation	Brush a fine skin of oil onto a baking tray and sprinkle with a little salt. Wash the potatoes thoroughly, halve them lengthways and press cut surfaces into the caraway. Place the potatoes cut face down on the baking tray and brush with olive oil. Bake in a medium oven (190 °C) for about 20 minutes.

You can also use herbes de Provence or sesame seeds instead of the caraway.

Carrot ragout

Preparation time	40 minutes

Ingredients		
	600 g (net weight)	carrots
	150 g (net weight)	potatoes, use the floury type
	1 small	leek
	1	onion
	2 tbsp (40 g)	olive oil
		marjoram
		thyme
		lovage
		parsley or chives
	½	bay leaf
		salt

Preparation   Wash and prepare the vegetables and cube (approx. 2 cm). Cut the leek diagonally into 1 cm slices and finely chop the onion. Sauté the onion and the leek in the olive oil, add the carrots and potatoes, briefly sauté together, add the spices and pour on about 300 ml water. Bring to the boil, cover and simmer until soft. The potatoes give a light binding. Season and serve with parsley or chives.

Vegetables

Celeriac with sour cream

Preparation time   30–40 minutes

Ingredients

2 (about 600 g)	celeriac
200 ml	sour cream
1	egg
	marjoram
	paprika powder
	salt
1	bay onion
½	bay leaf
1 tbsp	lemon juice

Preparation   Wash the celeriac, peel it and cut into approx. 1 cm slices. Boil the slices in salted water with a little lemon juice, the bay onion and the bay leaf until just soft. Butter a gratin dish and arrange the slices like overlapping roof tiles. Stir together the sour cream with the egg, spices and the salt, and pour over the vegetables. Cook swiftly au gratin in the oven (200 °C).

Chicory (Belgian, Brussels)

Bitter on the tongue, healthy for the stomach

Preparation time	30 minutes	
Ingredients	800 g	chicory (Belgian, Brussels)
	1 tbsp	leek
	1 tbsp	carrot
	1 tbsp	celeriac
	1 pinch	thyme
	1	clove
	2 tbsp (40 g)	butter
		vegetable stock
		salt
		parsley

Preparation
Make a cut 2–3 cm lengthways in the washed chicory stems. Those who prefer the chicory not too bitter can cut out a part of the stem. Blanch the chicory in salted water lightly acidified with lemon juice, rinse in cold water and drain. In the meantime cut the leek, carrot and celeriac into fine slices and sauté in the butter with the thyme and the clove. Place the chicory on top of this in a single layer, pour on some vegetable stock (to a depth of 1 cm) and lightly salt. Bring to the boil, then simmer on low heat until soft (about 20 minutes). Serve sprinkled with parsley.

Cream spinach

A classic accompaniment to fried egg

Preparation time	30 minutes

Ingredients		
	800 g	spinach
	300 ml	cream sauce (see recipe p. 21)
		salt
		nutmeg, freshly grated
	1 clove	garlic, finely squeezed
	1 tbsp	butter

Preparation Select spinach leaves and wash thoroughly. Heat in large pot with a little water until they shrink, then remove, drain and chop finely or pass through the mincer. Heat the cream sauce and add the spinach. Season with salt and nutmeg. Heat the butter and garlic together and, while still foaming hot, fold into the spinach.

Leaf spinach

Simple and good

Preparation time	20 minutes

Ingredients	800 g	spinach
	2 tbsp (40 g)	olive oil or butter
	1 clove	garlic, unpeeled and lightly pressed

Preparation   Select good leaves of spinach, wash thoroughly and drain a little, heat the oil and the garlic clove and add the spinach. On high heat allow to shrink down, while stirring, then salt, remove the garlic and serve. Depending on taste you can also add a little olive oil or fresh dill. If the spinach is somewhat bitter or tough, one can also cook it in plenty of salted water, and then serve with butter or olive oil.

Vegetables

Miller's wife aubergine

Preparation time	1 hour	
Ingredients	approx. 600 g	aubergines
	1	onion
		flour
		olive oil
		paprika powder
		herb salt
		salt
		parsley
	1	lemon

Preparation Prepare and wash the aubergines and cut lengthways into 1 cm slices. Salt the slices and leave to absorb for 20 minutes. In the meantime, peel the onion and slice into thin rings. Spice the rings with salt and paprika powder, dust them with flour, shake off excess and fry in olive oil until crisp and brown. Dab aubergines dry, season with herb salt and paprika powder, and fry in olive oil. Place on kitchen paper to remove excess fat. Arrange on plate, cover with onion rings, and garnish with parsley and lemon segments.

Lightly salted yoghurt with garlic and dill goes very well with this.

Nut parsnips

Preparation time   30 minutes

Ingredients

600 g (net weight)	parsnips
1	lemon, juice and finely grated peel
1–2	eggs
1 tbsp	flour
3 tbsp	hazelnuts, freshly grated
3 tbsp	white bread, freshly grated
	salt
	paprika powder
	butter oil (clarified) for frying

Preparation   Cut the parsnips lengthways into 6–8 mm slices and cook in salted water, lightly acidified with lemon juice, until just soft. Take out the parsnips and drain. Whisk the eggs and season with salt and paprika. Mix together the hazelnuts, grated lemon peel and white bread. First dust the parsnip slices in flour, brush off excess and then pass through the egg mix. Coat with the hazelnut mixture and fry in the butter oil on both sides until golden brown. Instead of butter oil you can use any other fat suitable for frying.

You can substitute celeriac for the parsnips, in which case, for a tasty variation, use almonds instead of hazelnuts.

Vegetables

Ratatouille

Moroccan aromas

Preparation time	30 minutes	
Ingredients	400 g	aubergines
	200 g	zucchini
	1	pepper, red
	1	pepper, yellow
	1 clove	garlic
	2 tbsp (40 g)	olive oil
	1 tsp	herbes de Provence
	1 tbsp	pinenuts
	1 tbsp	currants or raisins
		salt
		parsley, finely chopped

Preparation   Wash and prepare the vegetables and cut into approx. 2 cm pieces. Heat the olive oil, sauté the aubergines in it, add the zucchini, peppers, herbes de Provence and the unpeeled garlic clove, and briefly sauté them together. Pour on a very little vegetable stock, cover and simmer until soft. Shortly before dish is ready, add the pinenuts and the washed currants. Season and serve sprinkled with chopped parsley.

Red cabbage

Preparation time	1 hour	
Ingredients	500 g	red cabbage
	1 small	apple (Boskoop)
	1 small	onion
	1 tbsp (20 g)	butter
	1	herb pouch: bay leaf, clove, cinnamon stick, mustard seeds
	100 ml	apple juice
	100–200 ml	vegetable stock
		salt
	1 tsp	redcurrant or quince jelly
		lemon juice

Preparation
Finely chop or shave the cabbage. Peel the apple and cut into slices. Finely chop the onion. Sauté all together in the butter, add the herb pouch and pour on the apple juice and the vegetable stock. Cover and simmer on low heat until soft. Season with salt, add jelly and perhaps lemon juice.

Vegetables

Vegetable hotpot

A winter's delight

Preparation time	45 minutes	
Ingredients	600 g	vegetables, one type, such as: parsnips, white cabbage, chicory, fennel, etc.
	100 g	roast vegetables: equal portions of leeks, carrots and celeriac
		bay leaf (thyme, rosemary or caraway are also good)
	1–2 tbsp	butter or olive oil
	100–200 ml	vegetable stock
		salt
		parsley, finely chopped

Preparation Blanch the vegetable in salted water, cool quickly and drain. (There is no need to blanch root vegetables.) Lightly sauté the roast vegetables in butter or olive oil, place the vegetable on top, add salt and spices and pour on the vegetable stock. Bring to the boil, then cover and cook in medium oven, adding stock now and then. Serve sprinkled with parsley.

Vegetable piccata

Preparation time | 20 minutes + vegetable cooking time

Ingredients

600 g	vegetables: zucchini, chicory, celeriac, etc.
2	eggs
2 slices	white bread without crust, finely grated
1–2 tbsp	Parmesan cheese, freshly grated
3–4	sage leaves, finely chopped
1 tsp	parsley, finely chopped
1 pinch	paprika powder
	herb salt
	flour
1	lemon
	olive oil or butter oil

Preparation

Wash and prepare the vegetables (various types or just one) and boil in salted water until just soft. Leave to cool and cut into approx. 1 cm slices. Stir a thin mash with the eggs, Parmesan, white breadcrumbs, the finely chopped herbs and the paprika powder, and season with herb salt. Dust the vegetable slices in flour, brush off excess and dip in the coating. Brush off a little and fry in the hot oil or butter oil until golden brown. Place on kitchen paper to remove excess fat, and serve garnished with lemon quarters.

Vegetables

Zucchetti (zucchini)

Preparation time   15 minutes

Ingredients   800 g   zucchetti (young zucchini), small and fresh
                1 clove   garlic, finely squeezed
                               salt
                               pepper
                               oregano
                               parsley
                2 tbsp (40 g) olive oil

Preparation   Wash the zucchini and cut into slices or sticks. Heat the oil and sauté the zucchini and garlic in this. Add a little vegetable stock, cover and simmer on low flame for a few minutes until soft. Season with salt, pepper and oregano. Serve sprinkled with chopped parsley.

Nutmeg
Myristica fragrans

Nutmeg has great warmth and a good harmony of its forces. And when a man eats nutmeg, it does open his heart and purify his senses and bring him good reason. Take nutmeg and the same weight of cinnamon and a little of cloves, and pulverize this. And then, with this powder, and with breadcrumbs and a little water, make small cakes and eat these often; and this will diminish the bitterness of the heart and of your senses, and will open the heart and your dull senses, and it will make your spirit rejoice and purify your senses, and diminish all noxious juices in you; and it will lend your blood a goodly juice and render you strong.

Hildegard of Bingen

Doughs and mixes

Choux pastry

15 minutes

Ingredients

250 ml	milk
100 g	butter
1 tsp	cane sugar
1 tsp	lemon peel, finely grated
1 pinch	salt
150 g	semi-white flour, sieved
4	eggs, whisked

Preparation

Bring to the boil the milk with the butter, lemon peel, salt and sugar. Add all the flour at once and stir vigorously on low heat until a lump forms. Continue to stir for a short while until a light, white coating forms on the pan bottom (burn-off). Place the mix in a bowl and work in the eggs gradually, stirring vigorously. Cover until needed.

For savoury dishes, replace the lemon peel with nutmeg and a little pepper.

Doughs and mixes

Flan dough (cake dough)

For sweet and savoury

Preparation
time

10 minutes + 30 minutes standing time

Ingredients

200 g   wholemeal flour, preferably of freshly milled
                 wheat or spelt
100 g   butter, cut into cubes
50 ml   water
1 pinch   salt

Preparation   Put all the ingredients into a mixing bowl and knead together quickly.
                 Knead only until the dough sticks together as longer kneading makes
                 the dough tough. Form a ball and leave covered in a cold place for 30
                 minutes. Sufficient for a 30 cm diameter baking tray.

Quark filling

For filled vegetables, cannelloni, etc.

Preparation   10 minutes
time

Ingredients   300 g   quark (curd cheese), cottage cheese or ricotta
                1 tbsp   olive oil
                1   egg
                40 g   breadcrumbs
                1 tbsp   Parmesan cheese, freshly grated
                1 tbsp   herbs: thyme, parsley, sage
                1 tbsp   pinenuts, dry-roasted
                               herb salt

Preparation   Mix all ingredients together well and season with herb salt. Fill the veg-
                etables – cooked until just soft – and place in a gratin dish, pouring on a
                little vegetable stock. Bake in the oven at 200 °C for 20–25 minutes.

Doughs and mixes

Quark filo pastry

Many diverse uses

Preparation time	30 minutes

Ingredients		
	300 g	bread flour (wholemeal)
	240 g	butter, must be cold
	180 g	low-fat quark (curd cheese)
	5 g	salt

Preparation
Sieve the flour into a bowl. Cut the butter into small cubes and add to the flour with the quark. Quickly work together. The butter can remain in pieces in the dough. Cover the dough and place in fridge for 1 hour. You can use the dough like this, however it is better to roll it out into a 1 cm rectangle and fold it in three, then roll it out in the other direction into a rectangle and fold in four. Pack in foil and leave to cool for another hour.

Suitable for flans, tarts, cheese sticks, etc.

Quiche pastry

Preparation
time

5 minutes

Ingredients

30 g	semi-white flour, plain
30 g	cane sugar
3	eggs
300 ml	milk
1 pinch	salt
	cinnamon, as desired
	lemon peel, finely grated, as desired

Preparation

Blend all ingredients together – sufficient for a tart of 30 cm diameter. If you leave out the sugar, add a little more salt and replace the spices with herbs and nutmeg, the pastry is well suited for vegetable flans.

Doughs and mixes

198

Shortcrust (sweet)

A classic

Preparation time	10 minutes + 30 minutes standing time

Ingredients		
	175 g	semi-white flour, plain, finely milled – spelt is a good alternative
	100 g	butter, well cooled
	50 g	cane sugar
	1	egg yolk
	½	lemon, lemon peel (finely grated)
	1 pinch	salt

Preparation   Cut the butter into small cubes and add to the flour with the other ingredients. Prepare a shortcrust dough and leave to stand for about 30 minutes. Long kneading makes the dough tough!

Strudel dough

The basis for many tasty dishes

Preparation
time
15 minutes + 1–2 hours standing time

Ingredients

250 g	semi-white flour, plain
approx. 125 ml	water, depending on moistness of flour
1 small	egg
1 tbsp	sunflower oil
1 tsp	vinegar (cider vinegar)
1 pinch	salt

Preparation
Mix the flour with the other ingredients to form a dough, and knead until it shines like silk. Cover well and leave to stand at room temperature for at least 1 hour. The dough must not dry out.

Doughs and mixes

Yeast dough for pizzas

Preparation time | 10–15 minutes

Ingredients

300 g   bread flour (wholemeal)
150–200 ml   water, depending on flour
15 g   fresh yeast
1 tsp (6 g)   salt
50 g (50 ml)   olive oil

Preparation   Dissolve the yeast in a little water and make a starter with this and a little flour. As soon as the yeast froths up, add all the ingredients and knead to a smooth, soft dough. Leave at least 30 minutes before using.

Wild marjoram
Origanum vulgare

And he who has the red leprosy, whether newly or for a long time, let him take the juice of wild marjoram and somewhat less horehound juice, and let him also add oil of henbane thereto, more thereof than the other two, and also a little wine, and let him mix these together; and in a sweating bath he should salve himself with these fluids before going forth. And after he has risen from the bath, it will bring a sweat upon him, and therefore he should often salve himself straightaway with goat tallow that has melted in a bowl beside the fire, and lay himself in bed until he has grown dry. And after he is dry, let him also take wild marjoram again, and crush this, and add thereto wheat bran, and let him mix this in a warm bowl, and after the salving has dried let him place this warm upon the ulcers of the leprosy. And over this let him tie a binding, keeping it in place for upwards of one hour, so that it grows warm therefrom.

Hildegard of Bingen

203

Butter plait

For Sunday breakfast

Preparation time	20 minutes + standing time + baking time

Ingredients		
	500 g	semi-white flour (strong bread flour), sieved
	200 ml	milk, at room temperature
	20 g	fresh yeast
	1 tsp	sugar
	1	egg
	60 g	butter, soft
	10 g	salt
	1	egg, for brushing

Preparation — Sieve the flour into a bowl. Dissolve the yeast and sugar in the milk. Make a depression in the flour, and in this stir the milk mixture with a little flour, to make a thin starter dough. Leave until a light froth forms on the surface. Add the other ingredients and knead to form a smooth dough. Leave covered for 20 minutes. Divide the dough, form strands and braid a plait with these. Place on a baking tray, cover and leave for a further 30 minutes. Brush with egg and bake at 200° C for a good 30 minutes. You can also take the egg for brushing from the egg you add to the dough.

> If you place the plait in the fridge for 10 minutes before baking, it will rise still better.

Savoury pastries

Cabbage pierogi

<table>
<tr><td>Preparation time</td><td colspan="2">30 minutes + 40 minutes baking time</td></tr>
<tr><td>Ingredients</td><td>500 g</td><td>quark filo pastry (see recipe p. 197)</td></tr>
<tr><td></td><td>50 g</td><td>rice, already cooked</td></tr>
<tr><td></td><td>500 g</td><td>white cabbage, finely chopped</td></tr>
<tr><td></td><td>1 small</td><td>onion, finely chopped</td></tr>
<tr><td></td><td>½</td><td>chilli pepper, finely chopped</td></tr>
<tr><td></td><td>½ tbsp</td><td>mustard seeds</td></tr>
<tr><td></td><td>½ tbsp</td><td>caraway</td></tr>
<tr><td></td><td></td><td>salt</td></tr>
<tr><td></td><td>100 g</td><td>quark (curd cheese)</td></tr>
<tr><td></td><td>1</td><td>egg</td></tr>
<tr><td></td><td>100 ml</td><td>sour cream</td></tr>
<tr><td></td><td>1 tbsp</td><td>dill, finely chopped</td></tr>
<tr><td></td><td></td><td>salt</td></tr>
<tr><td></td><td></td><td>olive oil</td></tr>
</table>

Preparation   Sauté the onion in 1 tbsp olive oil, then add the cabbage, chilli pepper, mustard seeds and caraway and sauté together. Pour on a little water or vegetable stock, cover and stew on low heat until soft. When the cabbage is soft there should be no fluid left in the pan. Season with salt. In the meantime cover a 30 cm diameter baking tray with two thirds of the filo pastry so that the pastry extends about 1.5 cm over the edge. Prong it all over with a fork. Spread the rice on the pastry and place the cabbage on top of this. Mix the quark, egg, sour cream and dill, season with salt and pour on the cabbage. Fold the extending pastry over the filling and moisten with water. Roll out the rest of the pastry in a round shape and cover the dish with this, then press it firmly down. Prong with fork. Bake in a hot oven (200 °C) for about 40 minutes.

Caraway rolls

Makes about 30 snacks

Preparation time | 25 minutes + standing time for dough + 12 minutes baking time

Ingredients

200 g	bread flour (wholemeal)
100 g	butter
100 ml	cream
1 tsp	caraway, as desired
1 pinch	salt
1 small	egg
	caraway for sprinkling
	salt for sprinkling

Preparation

Mix together the flour with the butter, caraway and salt. Add the cream and quickly knead together. Knead as little as possible, or the dough becomes tough! Form a ball and cool in the fridge for at least 1 hour, preferably overnight. Roll out the dough with a little flour to form a square of 35 x 35 cm and cut out triangles of 10 cm side-length. Roll up from the lengthways side and place on a baking tray. Brush with whisked egg, sprinkle with caraway and salt, and cool again for 10 minutes. Bake in a preheated oven at 200 °C for 12–15 minutes. Serve warm with salad as hors d'oeuvre.

Savoury pastries

Cheese grills

Preparation time	20 minutes + 10 minutes baking time

Ingredients		
	1 large	onion
	1 tbsp	butter
	3	sage leaves
	20 g	butter
	20 g	semi-white flour, plain
	150 ml	milk
	150 g	grating cheese (Sbrinz, Gruyère or a tangy mountain cheese)
	1	egg
		salt
		nutmeg
		paprika
	6 slices	toasting bread

Preparation Peel the onion and cut into thin slices. Heat the tbsp of butter and sauté the sage leaves in this. Add the onion slices and roast on low heat until golden brown. In the meantime heat the rest of the butter and sweat the flour in it. Pour on the milk, bring to the boil while stirring, and make a thick béchamel sauce (5 minutes). Leave to cool a little, fold in the grated cheese and the egg, and season with freshly grated nutmeg and, if desired, with paprika powder. Spread thickly and pyramid-like on slices of bread, cover with the roasted onion rings, and grill in a hot oven (10 minutes).

Cheese sticks

Preparation time   15 minutes + cooling time + baking time

Ingredients   250 g   quark filo pastry (see recipe p. 197)
               1   egg yolk
               3 tbsp   Parmesan cheese
               1 pinch   paprika powder

Preparation   Roll out the pastry in a rectangle, about 5 cm thick. Brush with egg yolk. Blend the Parmesan cheese with the paprika powder and sprinkle half of this on the pastry. Press in a little with the rolling pin. Turn the pastry and do the same to the other side. Cut into 2 cm wide and 10 cm long strips. Twist the strips like a corkscrew and place on a baking tray. Cool for 10 minutes. Bake at 200–220 °C for about 12 minutes.

You can replace the cheese with caraway, sesame, poppy seeds, etc.

Savoury pastries

208

Cheese toasties

Small and tasty

Preparation
time

15 minutes + 10 minutes baking time

Ingredients	50 g	butter, at room temperature
	1	egg, at room temperature
	1	egg yolk, at room temperature
	150 g	Sbrinz cheese, freshly grated
		Tabasco
		marjoram or caraway
		herb salt
	6 slices	toasting bread

Preparation

Stir the butter until fluffy, beat in the egg and the egg yolk, and stir in the grated cheese. Season with Tabasco, marjoram and herb salt. Spread pyramid-like on slices of bread. Halve the slices diagonally, place on baking tray and bake in oven at 180–200 °C until golden brown, about 10 minutes. Goes very well with light vegetable soups.

Cream tartlets

Preparation time   20 minutes + 20 minutes baking time

Ingredients

500 g	quark filo pastry (see recipe p. 197)
200 ml	cream
20 g	flour
2	eggs
2 tbsp	herbs, chopped
	salt
	nutmeg, grated
	cayenne pepper

Preparation   Roll out the pastry 2–3 mm thick, cut out circles measuring 10 mm diameter, and fill suitable moulds with these. Leave in a cold place. Blend the cream, flour, eggs and herbs well with an egg whisk, and season with spices. Fill the tartlet moulds and bake at 200 °C for about 20 minutes.

> As variation you can also include diced and well-spiced vegetables (asparagus, leek, celery, etc.) in the mixture.

Savoury pastries

210

Feta tart

A taste of Greece

Preparation time	40 minutes + 20 minutes baking time

Ingredients		
	300 g	quark filo pastry (see recipe p. 197)
	200 g	feta cheese, finely cubed or crumbled
	50 g	olives, black and green, de-stoned and finely chopped
	1	chilli pepper, if desired de-seeded, and finely chopped
	1 tsp	basil, chopped
	1 tbsp	olive oil
	1 tbsp	breadcrumbs
		salt

Preparation   Roll out the dough thinly and cut out circles of 10 cm diameter. Mix the feta cheese with the other ingredients and if necessary season with salt. Lightly moisten the dough circles with water or egg white, and place about 1 tbsp of the filling on each. Close the dough over the filling and lightly press down the edges. Place on a baking tray lined with baking paper, and leave in a cold place for 10 minutes. Brush with egg and prong with fork. Bake for about 20 minutes at 200 °C.

You can also add pressed garlic and parsley or oregano to the filling.

Gnocchi quiche

Preparation time	40 minutes + 35 minutes baking time

Ingredients		
	300 g	quark filo pastry (see recipe p. 197)
	300 ml	cream sauce (see recipe p. 21)
	400 ml	water
	60 g	butter
	200 g	wholegrain semolina
	3	eggs
	100 g	Sbrinz cheese
		salt
	1 pinch	nutmeg
	1 tsp	parsley, finely chopped

Preparation   Bring to the boil the water with the butter and a pinch of salt. Reduce heat and add all the semolina at once, and cook while stirring until the mix comes free of the pot. Leave to cool a little and work in the eggs, parsley and Sbrinz cheese. Season with salt and nutmeg. Using a piping bag with a large spout or two spoons, form balls and put these in weakly boiling, lightly salted water and simmer for about 3–5 minutes until cooked. Take out and drain a little. Fill a cake tin of 30 cm diameter with the filo pastry and prong the bottom all over with a fork. Distribute the gnocchi on this and pour on the cream sauce. Sprinkle a tablespoon of grated Sbrinz or Parmesan over this, dribble on a little melted butter and bake for 35 minutes in a hot oven.

Savoury pastries

Leek quiche

Preparation time 40 minutes + 40 minutes baking time

Ingredients

300 g	quark filo pastry (see recipe p. 197)
1 kg	leek or onions, finely chopped
2 tbsp (50 g)	butter
	marjoram
	nutmeg
	Tabasco
	salt
50 g	Sbrinz cheese
250 ml	cream
3	eggs
	salt

Preparation

Wash the leeks and cut into 1 cm strips. Heat the butter and sauté the leeks in this. Cover and simmer for 30 minutes on low heat until cooked. If necessary, pour on a little vegetable stock. Season with marjoram, Tabasco and salt, and leave to cool a little. Lightly sprinkle a 30 cm diameter baking tray with flour and fill this with the dough. Prong the bottom with a fork. Spread the leeks on this. Whisk together the eggs, cream and Sbrinz cheese, and season with a little salt. Pour over the leeks and bake at 200 °C for about 35 minutes.

213

Spinach quiche

Italian recipe

Preparation time | 20 minutes + 35 minutes baking time

Ingredients

300 g	quiche dough (see recipe p. 198)
250 g	ricotta or whole-milk quark (curd cheese)
500 g	spinach
50 g	Parmesan cheese, freshly grated
1 (50 g)	onion
1 clove	garlic
1 small	chilli pepper
2 stalks	basil
½ bunch	parsley
	salt

Preparation

Roll out dough, fill a 30 cm diameter tray and prong all over with fork. Wash the spinach and drain a little. Place in pot on high heat and shrink, then remove and place to drain in sieve. Chop. Dice the onion, garlic and chilli pepper (possibly removing seeds), and sauté in the olive oil. Finely chop the basil and parsley. Mix all ingredients and season with salt. Spread on the base. Bake at 200 °C for about 30 minutes.

Savoury pastries

Squash quiche

Preparation time 30 minutes + 35 minutes baking time + standing time

Ingredients

Dough:
200 g	wholemeal flour (wheat or spelt flour)
100 g	butter cubes
50 ml	cold water
4 g	salt

Filling:
800 g (net weight)	squash ('Hokkaido', 'Potimarron')
1 tsp	ginger, fresh, finely grated
1 tsp	curry powder
20 g	butter or olive oil
2 tbsp	sesame seeds
2	eggs
200 ml	cream
	salt
	dill and Tabasco, as desired

Preparation To make the dough, quickly mix together the butter and flour and knead together with salt and water. Kneading too long makes the dough tough! Leave covered in the fridge for at least 40 minutes or overnight.

Coarsely grate the squash. Heat the butter and briefly sauté the ginger in this. Add the squash, sauté together, add the curry powder and roast a little. Salt, cover and sauté until semi-soft in its own juice. You may need to add 1–2 tbsp water. Dry-roast the sesame until the aroma is released. Add to the squash. Fill a 30 cm diameter quiche dish with the dough, prong with fork and spread the cooled squash on this. Blend together the eggs and cream, season with salt and spices, and pour over the squash. Bake at 200 °C in the bottom of the oven for about 35 minutes.

As variation, you can mix in small cubes of feta cheese instead of the sesame seeds.

215

Vegetable toast

Seasonal variations

Preparation time	30 minutes + 10 minutes baking time

Ingredients		
	1 l	vegetable stock
	8 slices	toasting bread, white or wholemeal
	16 slices	raclette cheese
	4	chicory (Belgian, Brussels) or similar quantity of fennel, zucchini, celeriac, spinach, etc.
	2 tbsp (40 g)	butter, at room temperature
	1 tsp	mustard
		herb salt
	1 tsp	parsley, finely chopped

Preparation   Wash the chicory and cut lengthways, then cook in the vegetable stock until just soft. Remove and drain. Blend the butter with the mustard until smooth, and spread this on the bread slices. Lightly flatten the chicory halves (with a meat tenderizer) and place on the bread slices. Sprinkle with parsley and a little herb salt. Place the cheese slices on top and bake au gratin at 200 °C for about 10 minutes.

Savoury pastries

Williams toast

Preparation time	30 minutes	
Ingredients	8 slices	toasting bread
	3 tbsp	mayonnaise
	2	eggs, hard-boiled
	4 large	pears
	16 slices	raclette cheese
		paprika powder
	½ tsp	parsley, finely chopped
	1	bay leaf
	½ stick	cinnamon
		pear purée, as desired
	½	lemon, juice and peel

Preparation — Peel and halve the pears and remove seeds. Poach until soft in water sweetened with the pear purée, together with the bay leaf, cinnamon and lemon juice and peel. Leave to cool a little in the liquid. Remove and drain. Cut pears in fan-shape pattern. Peel the eggs, chop and mix with the mayonnaise. Spread on the bread slices, put the pears on top and cover with the cheese slices. Bake au gratin in hot oven (200 °C). Serve sprinkled with paprika powder and finely chopped parsley.

Sage
Salvia officinalis

Sage is warm and dry by nature, and it grows more in consequence of the sun's heat than in consequence of the earth's moisture. And it is useful against sick juices because it is dry. Both raw and cooked it is good to eat for those plagued by noxious juices, for it does suppress them. Then take sage, and pulverize it, and eat this powder with bread, and it will diminish the superfluity of bad juices in you. And he who suffers some filthy smell, let him place sage in his nose and it will help him.

But he who has superfluity of rheum, or he who has stinking breath, let him cook sage in wine and then let him strain the same through a cloth and drink this often, and the bad juices and the rheum in him will lessen.

And if he who has these ailments suffers somewhat from gout, then let him cook sage in water and drink it, and the juices and the rheum will be lessened.

And if he who has these ailments suffers somewhat from palsy, then let him cook sage in water as was described, and let him drink this, and if its warmth is moderated with water, then it will suppress the palsy in a man. For he who would give sage to this man with wine, the wine would make the palsy juices exceed their bounds in him. And he who has no desire to eat, let him take sage and somewhat less chervil, and some garlic, and let him crush these together in vinegar, and make therefrom a spice; and let him dip the food that he desires to eat in this, and he will have an appetite to eat.

Hildegard of Bingen

Almond apple pie

Sponge

Preparation time	30 minutes + baking time	
Ingredients	180 g	cane sugar, organic, raw, finely milled
	125 g	butter
	4	egg yolks
	180 g	semi-white flour, plain
	1 tbsp	baking powder
	½	lemon peel, finely grated
	1 pinch	salt
	4	egg whites
	50 g	almond flakes
	4	apples, e.g. Reinette (similar to Russet)

Preparation Cream together the butter and sugar until light and fluffy. Stir in the egg yolks. Sieve the flour with the baking powder and fold into the mix with the lemon peel. Whip the egg whites, plus the salt, until stiff, and carefully fold in. Place in a greased, breadcrumb-sprinkled 24 cm diameter cake tin. Peel and halve the apples, and remove the seeds. Cut biscuit incisions into the round side and place on the dough with the cut side uppermost. Sprinkle on the almond flakes and bake at about 170 °C for 40 minutes. Test with skewer to see if done.

Also tastes good with pears.

Apple cake

Preparation   30 minutes + baking time
time

Ingredients   1 batch   cake dough (quiche pastry, see recipe p. 198)
                 800 g   apples
                 120 g   cane sugar
                 50 g   raisins
                 50 g   hazelnuts, grated
                 1 tbsp (20 g)   semi-white flour, plain
                 100 ml   milk
                 100 ml   cream
                 2   eggs
                 1 knife tip   cinnamon
                 ½   lemon peel, finely grated
                 1 pinch   salt

Preparation   Line a 30 cm diameter quiche dish with the pastry. Peel, halve and core
                 the apples. Grate coarsely, and mix with sugar, raisins and the grated
                 hazelnuts. Add to the pastry. Blend together the other ingredients and
                 pour on the apple. Bake at 180 °C for 35 to 40 minutes. Glaze with
                 quince jelly while still hot.

Make sure there is sufficient underheat!

Apple strudel

Preparation time	30 minutes + baking time	

Ingredients	1 kg (net weight)	apples
	approx. 100 g	cane sugar, depending on type of apples
	120 g	raisins
	½ tsp	cinnamon
	½ tsp	lemon peel, finely grated
	60 g	butter
	150 g	breadcrumbs
	60 g	pinenuts or lightly roasted, grated hazelnuts
	20 g	butter for brushing
	300 g	strudel dough (see recipe p. 200)

Preparation   Slice the apples finely and mix with the sugar, cinnamon, raisins and lemon peel. Roast the pinenuts and the breadcrumbs in the butter, stirring continually, until golden brown. Carefully roll out the strudel dough to a skin-thin rectangle on a flour-sprinkled tea towel. Sprinkle the breadcrumb mixture on a third of the surface and place the apples on top. Roll up with the aid of the tea towel, and place on a tray lined with baking paper. Brush with melted butter and bake at moderate heat for about 40 minutes. Cut open and serve with vanilla sauce while still warm.

The strudel is even crispier if you brush melted butter on the stretched dough before putting on the filling.

Sweet pastries

Carrot cake

Preparation   30 minutes + 50 minutes baking time
time

Ingredients   5   eggs
               250 g   cane sugar
               250 g (net weight)   carrots, finely shredded
               250 g   almonds, finely grated
               1   lemon, juice and peel
               90 g   flour
               1 tbsp   baking powder
               1 pinch   salt

Preparation   Separate the eggs and beat with the sugar until light and fluffy. Add all
               the ingredients one after another in the sequence above, and mix. Beat
               the egg white, plus pinch of salt, until stiff, and fold into the mix. Butter a
               24 cm diameter cake tin and sprinkle with breadcrumbs. Fill with the mix
               and bake at 180 °C for about 50 minutes.

Chocolate cake

Preparation   20 minutes + 1 hour baking time
time

Ingredients   140 g   butter
                250 g   cane sugar
                6   eggs
                140 g   chocolate, and some melted for glazing
                250 g   hazelnuts or almonds, finely grated
                2 tbsp   cherry brandy
                50 g   semi-white flour
                20 g   baking powder
                3 tbsp   cranberry jam

Preparation   Beat together the room-temperature butter with the sugar until light and
                fluffy. Separate the eggs and stir in the egg yolks one at a time. Mix in
                the chocolate, hazelnuts and the cherry brandy. Sieve the flour with the
                baking powder and also mix in. Whip the egg white, plus pinch of salt,
                until stiff, and carefully fold into the mix. Line a cake tin with baking paper
                and grease the sides. Place the mix in the tin. Bake at 180–200 °C for
                about 50–60 minutes, with open steam vent (test with skewer). Remove
                the cake from the tin and turn upside down to cool on a metal rack. After
                cooling, cut in half, spread the cranberry jam on one surface, then put
                cake together again. Glaze with chocolate.

Sweet pastries

Coconut cake

Preparation time	30 minutes + 40 minutes baking time	
Ingredients	250 g	butter
	250 g	cane sugar, finely milled
	5	eggs
	250 g	semi-white flour
	125 g	shredded coconut
	500 ml	milk
	3 pods	cardamom
	2 cm	cinnamon sticks

Preparation   Stir the butter with the sugar until light and fluffy. Separate the eggs and stir the egg yolk into the butter-sugar mix. Sieve the flour and fold into the butter-sugar mix together with the shredded coconut. Whip the egg white, plus pinch of salt, until stiff, and fold into the mixture. Butter a cake tin (24 cm) and fill with the mixture. Bake for about 40 minutes at 180 °C (skewer test). Crush the cardamom pods and add to the milk with the cinnamon. Heat but do not boil. Then pour one tbsp at a time over the still warm cake and allow it to be absorbed.

Crumble cake

Preparation time   40 minutes

Ingredients

Dough:

20 g	fresh yeast
150 ml	milk
300 g	wholemeal spelt flour, freshly milled
2 tbsp	honey
1	egg
1 tsp	lemon peel, finely grated
1 pinch	salt
40 g	butter

Crumble:

200 g	apples, grated
175 g	strong white flour
75 g	cane sugar
100 g	butter
½ tsp	cinnamon
½ tsp	baking powder
1 pinch	salt

Preparation   Dissolve the yeast in a little milk. Place the spelt flour in a bowl and form a depression, pouring in the yeast and mixing it with a little of the flour. The mixture should still be almost fluid. Cover and leave to froth up. Add the other ingredients up to and including the butter, and knead for 10 minutes into a soft, elastic dough. Cover and leave to rise for 20–30 minutes. For the crumble part of the recipe, blend the 175 g of flour, the cane sugar, butter, cinnamon, baking powder and salt in an electric blender, until you get a crumblike consistency. If need be, add a little milk. Roll out the dough and line a greased and floured, 30 cm diameter tin with it. Sprinkle with the grated apple, and spread the crumble evenly on top. Leave to rise for 1 hour, and bake at 200–220 °C for about 30 minutes. The cake is particularly fine if you dribble melted butter on top after baking. After cooling, cut into slices. Serve sprinkled with icing sugar.

Sweet pastries

226

Easter cake

Tasty at other times too

Preparation time	1 ½ hours

Ingredients		
	300 g	shortcrust pastry (see recipe p. 199)
	500 ml	milk
	100 g	risotto rice (Arborio, Baldo)
	1 pinch	salt
	3	egg yolks
	100 g	sugar
	100 g	quark (curd cheese)
	50 ml	cream
	50 g	currants
	1	lemon, finely grated peel
	100 g	almonds, finely grated
	3	egg whites, beaten stiff

Preparation — Cook the rice with the milk and the salt, stirring occasionally. Line a 26 cm diameter cake tin with the pastry and prong the bottom with a fork. Stir together the sugar and egg yolks until fluffy, then fold in the quark and cream. Add the currants, lemon peel and almonds, and mix well. Fold in the egg whites and the fully cooled rice, and fill a prepared tin with the mixture. Bake for 10 minutes at 220 °C, then reduce temperature to 200 °C and bake the cake for a further 30 minutes. If needed, cover the cake near the end of baking with aluminium foil (to prevent burning). After cooling, sprinkle with icing sugar.

Hélène ring cake

An Alsace speciality

Preparation time	2–3 hours

Ingredients		
	500 g	semi-white flour, plain
	10 g	fresh yeast
	300 ml	milk
	100 g	butter, soft
	1	egg
	50 g	sugar
	½ tsp	salt
	100 g	raisins (Malaga)
	50 g	currants
	50 g	almonds, coarsely chopped
	approx. 20	almonds, to line the tin

Preparation   Sieve the flour into a mixing bowl. Dissolve the yeast in 100 ml of milk and make a thin starter in the bowl with a little flour. Once the starter has frothed up, add the rest of the milk, and the butter, egg, sugar and salt, and knead until the dough shines like silk and comes free of the bowl. Cover and leave to rise until doubled in volume. In the meantime, soak the raisins and currants in water (approx. 20 minutes) and then pour off and drain well. Generously butter a medium ring-cake mould and line with the whole almonds. When the dough has risen, knead in the raisins, currants and chopped almonds, and fill the tin. Cover with a cloth and leave to rise again until double in volume. Then bake at 175 °C for approx. 50–60 minutes. After baking turn out onto a metal rack and leave to cool.

Sweet pastries

228

Maple croissants

With tea or coffee

Preparation time	20 minutes + baking time	
Ingredients	200 g	wholemeal wheat flour, if possible freshly milled
	50 g	buckwheat flour
	150 g	butter from the fridge
	150 g	almonds, freshly grated
	100 ml	maple syrup
	1 tsp	lemon peel, finely grated
	1 knife tip	vanilla powder
	1 pinch	salt
	1–2 tbsp	buttermilk or egg yolk

Preparation: Place wholemeal wheat flour and buckwheat flour in a mixing bowl. Cut the butter into small cubes and add to the flour with the other ingredients. Knead quickly and leave in a cold place for 30 minutes. Form 1 cm thick rolls and cut these into 3 cm long pieces, then form these into croissant shapes and place on a baking tray lined with baking paper. If the dough sticks, rub a little oil into your hands. Bake at 180 °C for about 10 minutes. After cooling, store in a tin.

Nest of peaches

Quick and delicious

Preparation time	20 minutes + 20 minutes baking time	

Ingredients	1 batch	quark filo pastry (see recipe p. 197)
	4 halves	peaches, preserved or freshly cooked
	2 tbsp	almonds, finely grated
	1 tsp	honey or pear purée
	a little	lemon juice
	a little	lemon peel, finely grated
	1 pinch	cinnamon
	1	egg, if desired (not essential)
	1 tbsp	redcurrant jelly, warmed
	3	pistachios, shelled and chopped

Preparation	Roll out the pastry 6 mm thick and cut out circular pieces of 8–9 cm diameter with a serrated cutter. Place on baking tray. Mix together the almonds with the honey, cinnamon, lemon juice and lemon peel. This should give a firm but still spreadable mix. If necessary, moisten with a little cooking water from stewing the fruit. Fill the peach halves with this mix and place on dough, cut face downwards. Brush the sides with egg and bake for 20 minutes at approx. 180 °C. After baking, glaze with redcurrant jelly and sprinkle with a few chopped pistachios.

Sweet pastries

Quark cakes

Preparation   20 minutes + baking time
time

Ingredients   1 batch   shortcrust pastry (see recipe p. 199)
                  500 g   low-fat quark
                  100 g   cane sugar
                  4   egg yolks
                  100 g   butter, melted
                  50 g   flour
                  ½   lemon peel
                  100 g   currants
                  1 tbsp   rosewater
                  4   egg whites
                  50 g   sugar

Preparation   Marinate the currants in the rosewater. Line a 24 cm diameter cake tin
                  with the shortcrust pastry. Place aluminium foil or tissue paper on top, and
                  fill with cherry stones or peas (to weight paper). Bake blind at 180 °C
                  for 20 minutes. Remove from oven and take out cherry stones and the
                  paper/foil. In the meantime blend well the quark, cane sugar, egg yolk,
                  butter, flour, lemon peel and currants. Beat the egg whites with the sugar
                  until stiff and shiny and carefully fold into the quark mix. Fill on top of
                  the pre-baked bottom and bake for 50–60 minutes at 120–130 °C.
                  Skewer test. Tastes best when served lukewarm accompanied by
                  crushed and sugared raspberries.

Raisin fingers

Small and tasty

Preparation time	30 minutes + standing time + baking time

Ingredients		
	50 g	raisins
	50 g	currants
	90 g	butter
	90 g	cane sugar, raw, organic, finely milled, or icing sugar
	1	egg
	1 pinch	salt
	200 g	semi-white flour
	1 knife tip	vanilla powder
	a little	egg white
	a little	lemon juice

Preparation   Wash the currants and raisins, soak for 20 minutes and drain in sieve. Stir together the butter and sugar until light and fluffy, then stir in the egg. Mix in the flour, salt, raisins and currants, then place the dough in a cool place for about 30 minutes. Form 'fingers' no bigger than 1 cm, and cut diagonal sections from these, 4 cm in length. Place on a tray lined with baking paper, and bake for about 10 minutes at 180 °C. Blend the icing sugar with lemon juice and egg white to a smooth consistency, and spread this on the still hot fingers. Store in tins after cooling.

Sweet pastries

232

Redcurrant cake

A Swedish recipe

Preparation time	30 minutes + baking time

Ingredients

1 batch	shortcrust pastry (see recipe p. 199)
250 g	redcurrants, de-stalked and weighed
75 g	butter
100 g	cane sugar
2	egg yolks
100 g	almonds, finely grated
200 ml	cream

Preparation   Line a 30 cm diameter cake tin with the shortcrust pastry and prong the bottom with a fork. Beat the butter and sugar together until light and fluffy, stir in the egg yolk and fold in the grated almonds. Mix in 100 g of the redcurrants, distributing these evenly through the mixture. Bake at 175 °C for 30–35 minutes. Leave to cool and remove from tin. Whip the cream until stiff and spread on the cake. Sprinkle the rest of the berries on top.

Cinnamon
Cinnamomum verum

Cinnamon is also very warm and has strong forces, and also holds moderate moisture within it. But its warmth is so strong that it does suppress that moisture, and in him who often eats it, it diminishes the noxious juices and prepares good juices in him.

Hildegard of Bingen

Alsace apricots

Preparation
time

1 hour

Ingredients

Choux pastry:
250 ml	milk
100 g	butter
1 tsp	lemon peel, grated
1 tsp	cane sugar
1 pinch	salt
150 g	semi-white flour
4	eggs, whisked
approx. 1 tsp	decorating sugar

Apricot filling:
10	apricots
	cane sugar, quantity depending on sweetness of apricots
20 g	butter
100 ml	cream, whipped until stiff

Preparation

Boil up the milk with butter, lemon peel, salt and sugar. Add the sieved flour in one go, and stir vigorously on low heat with a wooden spatula until it forms a homogenous lump. Continue to stir briefly until a light, white coating forms on the bottom of the pan. Put the mixture in a bowl and gradually work in the eggs, stirring vigorously.

For the cream puff, place walnut size balls of the mix with a spoon, or using a piping bag, on a baking tray lined with baking paper. Brush with an egg and water mix. Sprinkle with decorating sugar, and bake for about 20 minutes at 200 °C. Turn out onto a metal rack to cool.

De-stone the washed apricots and cut into 1 cm cubes. Mix the cubes with sugar and the melted butter. Place on a baking tray and bake until soft in a hot oven. The cubes should remain whole. Cut a puff in half and fill the lower part with the cooled apricots. Garnish with whipped cream and replace the top.

Sweet puddings and desserts

Apple crumble

Preparation time	1 hour	
Ingredients	600 g	apples
	1 tbsp	sugar
	1 tbsp	lemon juice
	50 g	flour
	30 g	oatflakes
	100 g	cane sugar
	50 g	butter
	½ tsp	cinnamon
	20 g	almond flakes

Preparation	Peel, halve and core the apples and cut into approx. 5 mm slices. Place in overlapping roof-tile pattern on a buttered gratin dish, brush with lemon juice, then sprinkle with sugar.
	Mix together the ingredients for the crispy mix until they form a crumbly consistency, and spread this over the apples. Bake at 180 °C for 30–40 minutes. Serve lukewarm.

For special occasions you can serve with a light and airy vanilla sauce (see recipe p. 259) or half-whipped cream.

Apple snow

Deliciously airy

Preparation time	20 minutes

Ingredients		
	400 g	apples, Reinette (similar to Russet) are very good
	2 tbsp	lemon juice
	100 ml	cream
	2	egg whites
	50 g	sugar
	1 small pinch	salt

Preparation   Peel, halve and core the apples, and marinate in the lemon juice. Whip the cream until semi-stiff. Whisk the egg white until stiff with sugar and salt. Finely grate the apples directly into the cream, add the rest of the lemon juice and immediately mix with the cream, and fold in the egg white. Arrange in dessert dishes, garnish with apple slices and serve. The apple snow has to be eaten fairly quickly.

Sweet puddings and desserts

Apple-cream sauce

A Lukas Klinik speciality

Preparation time	15 minutes	
Ingredients	500 g	apple quince purée
	25 g	bitter chocolate
	50 g	pumpernickel
	150 ml	cream
Preparation	Put the apple sauce in a bowl or in several portion-size dishes. Grate the chocolate and pumpernickel coarsely and sprinkle on the apple sauce. Whip the cream until stiff and garnish the dessert generously with it.	

Apple-juice cream

A taste for all seasons

Preparation time	20 minutes + time to soak

Ingredients		
	300 ml	apple juice
	50 g	cane sugar
	1 tbsp	lemon juice
	1 pinch	salt
	1	egg yolk
	25 g	cornflour
	100 ml	apple juice
	100 ml	cream
	1	egg white

Preparation — Bring to the boil the first quantity of apple juice with the sugar, lemon juice and salt. Stir the egg yolk with the rest of the apple juice and the cornflour until smooth, and then stir into the simmering fluid. Bring to the boil while stirring, pass through a sieve and leave to cool inside a bowl of water, stirring from time to time. Whip the cream and the egg white until stiff, and fold into the dessert. Serve sprinkled with cinnamon sugar.

Also worth trying with blackcurrant or grape juice.

Cherry and millet quark

Light and tasty millet

Preparation time	40 minutes + millet cooking time

Ingredients		
	40 g	millet
	250 ml	milk
	½ tsp	lemon peel, finely grated
	1 pinch	salt
	200 g	quark (whole-milk)
	300 g	cherries (the small, black type are very good)
		pear purée for sweetening
	1 tbsp	hazelnuts, roasted and coarsely crushed

Preparation Preferably the day before, blanch the millet in boiling water, pour off liquid, rinse in cold water and drain. Bring to the boil with the milk, a pinch of salt and the lemon peel, then simmer until soft. After this has cooled, mix the quark with it, fold in the de-stoned cherries and sweeten as desired. Arrange in bowls and sprinkle with the hazelnuts. Cinnamon sugar also goes very well with this.

Chestnut cream

Preparation
time

20 minutes

Ingredients

300 g   chestnut purée (ready-made)
½ batch   vanilla sauce (see recipe p. 259)
100 ml   cream, whipped
            fruit to garnish

Preparation

Stir the chestnut purée with the vanilla sauce until smooth. Fold in the whipped cream, arrange the dessert in bowls and garnish with fruit (quince compote, pomegranate seeds).

Sweet puddings and desserts

Chocolate cream

Preparation time   20 minutes

Ingredients   vanilla cream (see recipe p. 258)
            75 g   chocolate, rich, dark

Preparation The same method as for vanilla cream, but with only 30 g sugar. Melt 75 g of the chocolate in the still-hot cream, stirring as you do so, until the chocolate has completely fused with the cream.

Cinnamon cream

The basis for many creations

Preparation time	30 minutes + cooling time

Ingredients	400 ml	milk
	1	cinnamon stick, crumbled
	⅓	vanilla pod, split lengthways
	1 pinch	salt
	35 g	rice flour
	2 tbsp	maple syrup
	100 ml	cream

Preparation Bring to boil 300 ml of the milk with the cinnamon, vanilla and salt. Stir the rice flour with the rest of the milk until smooth, then stir into the boiling fluid. Bring back to the boil, then turn off heat, cover and leave to absorb for 10 minutes. Pass through sieve and sweeten with maple syrup. Place in separate bowl of water to cool, stirring occasionally. Whip the cream and fold into the dessert. Garnish with fruit.

> All types of sugared berries or sauces go very well with this pudding.

Crème Arabia

Quick as a flash

Preparation time	10 minutes

Ingredients	350 g	quark (curd cheese), whole-milk
	75 g	cane sugar
	1 knife tip	vanilla powder
	100 ml	coffee: boil up 100 ml water with 15 g coffee, then strain
	100 ml	cream
		milk, as required

Preparation Stir the quark with the sugar, coffee and vanilla powder until fluffy. Depending on the consistency of the quark, you may need to add a little milk. Whip the cream until stiff and fold into the mix. Serve garnished with chocolate shavings or a little whipped cream (kept back).

Dried fruit compote

From the good old days

Preparation time	20 minutes + soaking time

Ingredients	300 g	dried fruit: apricots, pears, figs, prunes, etc.
	300 ml	water
	½	cinnamon stick
	½	bay leaf
	1	clove
	2	cardamom
	1 tsp	cornflour or kuzu (root starch), binds very finely pear purée as required

Preparation Wash the fruit and chop as desired. Soften in water for about 3 hours. Drain, and keep the water. Add the spices and bring to the boil. Stir the cornflour with a little water until smooth in consistency, and stir into the boiling fluid. Bring to the boil again and pour over the fruit. Sweeten to taste and leave to cool.

Sweet puddings and desserts

Fruit quark

Preparation time   10–20 minutes

Ingredients   250 g   quark (curd cheese), whole-milk milk, depending
                            on quark consistency
               2–3 tbsp   pear purée
               500 g   seasonal fruit
                            lemon juice to taste

Preparation   Mix the quark with the milk to an airy and smooth consistency. Mix in the
               chopped fruit, and add pear purée, and if necessary also lemon juice to
               taste. Roasted, roughly chopped hazelnuts go very well with this.

Madrid pears

Preparation time	30 minutes + cooling time	
Ingredients	2 large	pears
	500 ml	grape juice (red)
	1	cinnamon stick
	½	lemon, the juice
	2–3 tbsp	cane sugar
	2 g	agar-agar
	100 ml	cream
	1 tsp	brittle (sweet made from fragmented nuts)

Preparation   Wash, peel and core the pears. Bring to the boil the grape juice with the cinnamon, lemon juice, lemon peel and sugar. Add the pear halves and simmer gently. You may need to turn them to ensure they colour uniformly. Allow them to cool in the stewing juice. Remove and drain. Strain off 200 ml of the stewing liquid and mix together with the agar-agar. Leave to swell for 5 minutes and then bring to the boil while stirring. Make fan-shaped cuts in the pears and arrange in dessert dishes. Pour on the still warm liquid and leave to cool. Garnish with whipped cream and the brittle.

Millet bake with apples

Preparation time	25 minutes + 40 minutes baking time	

Ingredients	80 g	millet
	500 ml	milk
	1 tsp	lemon peel, finely grated
	1 pinch	salt
	1	egg yolk
	100 g	cane sugar
	600 g	apples
	1	egg white

Preparation Blanch the millet in boiling water, pour off liquid, rinse in cold water and drain. Bring to the boil with the milk, cover, reduce to lowest heat and leave to swell for 15 minutes. In the meantime stir the egg yolk and the sugar together until light and fluffy. Peel the apples, grate them and add them to the egg yolk mixture with the lemon peel. Add the millet and mix well together. Whip the egg white until stiff and carefully fold in. Place in a greased baking tin and bake for 35–40 minutes at 170–180 °C. Vanilla sauce (see recipe p. 259) goes very well with this.

Orange cream

Well worth the effort

Preparation time	30 minutes + cooling time

Ingredients		
	75 g	rice, preferably risotto rice
	300 ml	water
	1	vanilla powder or a small piece of vanilla pod
	½	orange, the peel (zest), finely grated
	1 pinch	salt
	250 g	oranges, peeled then weighed
	60 g	pear purée, depending on acidity of oranges
	150 ml	cream
		cinnamon sugar for the garnish

Preparation

Cook the well-washed and drained rice with the water, vanilla, orange peel and salt until soft, then leave to cool. Peel the oranges with a sharp knife, also removing the white pith. Then cube the fruit and mix with the rice, along with the exuded juice. Sweeten with pear purée. Whip the cream and fold into the mix. Distribute to dessert bowls and serve sprinkled with cinnamon sugar.

The dessert can also be decorated with slivers of orange and whipped cream. Also tastes good with pineapple, cherries or mixed fruit.

Sweet puddings and desserts

Paska

Russian Easter dessert (gives about 10 portions)

Preparation time	1 hour	
Ingredients	750 g	low-fat quark (curd cheese)
	100 g	butter
	100 g	cane sugar
	200 ml	cream
	25 g	raisins
	25 g	currants
	25 g	almonds, peeled
	1 knife tip	vanilla powder
	1 tbsp	rosewater

Preparation · Place the quark in a tea towel and press; 500 g should be left over after this. Wash and dry the raisins and currants and mix with the rosewater. Chop the almonds coarsely and roast until light brown. Beat together the sugar and the butter until light and fluffy. Add the quark and stir together. Add the dry fruits, the vanilla and the almonds. Whip the cream until stiff, add and mix everything together well. Line a perforated cylindrical tin (cheese tin) with a tea towel and fill it with the mixture. Fold the tea towel over the top and secure with a weight. Leave in the fridge for one day. Remove from the tin, remove the tea towel and cut into pieces. Serve with dried fruit compote (see recipe p. 246).

Quark cream with berries

Lots of uses

Preparation time	10 minutes

Ingredients		
	250 g	quark (curd cheese), whole-milk
	2–4 tbsp	milk, depending on the consistency of the quark
	2 tbsp	pear purée
	250 g	berries: blueberries, raspberries, etc. or a mixture
		lemon juice to taste

Preparation	Stir the quark with the milk and pear purée until smooth. Fold in the berries and add lemon juice to taste

Sweet puddings and desserts

Red tapioca

A northern speciality

Preparation
time
30 minutes

Ingredients
400 ml	fruit juice (half raspberries, half redcurrants)
60 g	tapioca (sago)
200 ml	water
	cane sugar as desired
100 ml	cream

Preparation
Soak the tapioca in the water for 15 minutes. Bring the fruit juice mixture to the boil, stir in the tapioca and cook while stirring frequently, until the tapioca is soft and transparent. Sweeten with the cane sugar and pour into small tins rinsed in cold water. Turn out after cooling. Garnish with berries and serve the cooled cream separately as accompaniment.

Rice pudding

Delicious with raspberry sauce

Preparation time	50 minutes + baking time

Ingredients

500 ml	milk
½	vanilla pod
75 g	risotto rice (Arborio, Baldo)
1 pinch	salt
1	egg
40 g	sugar
20 g	butter

Preparation   Rinse the rice in first hot and then cold water, and drain. Bring to the boil the rice and milk with the vanilla pod (cut open) and the pinch of salt, and simmer on low heat for 35 minutes until soft. If necessary, dilute with a little milk. Fold sugar and egg into the mixture with a whisk and fill a buttered baking tin. Cover with flakes of butter and bake the pudding in a water tray in the oven, until golden yellow. Baking time about 35 minutes at 200 °C.

Sweet puddings and desserts

Semolina timbales

Preparation time   20 minutes

Ingredients   300 ml   milk
               100 ml   water
               10 g   butter
               20 g   cane sugar
               1 pinch   salt
               50 g   semolina (durum wheat)
               20 g   currants
               ½   lemon, the peel

Preparation   Bring to the boil the milk with the water, butter, sugar, lemon peel and salt. Stir in the semolina, bring to the boil and cook on low heat for 5 minutes. Fold in the washed and dried currants. Rinse small timbale (cone or thimble-shaped) moulds in cold water, fill them with the mix and leave to cool. To turn out, cut round edge with knife. Serve with a fruit sauce.

Spiced apples

Preparation time — 15 minutes + cooking time

Ingredients

600 g (4)	apples: Marigold, Reinette or Russet, Golden Delicious
1	cinnamon stick
2–3	cardamoms, lightly crushed
10 cm	orange peel (zest)
10 cm	lemon peel
3–4 grains	allspice
150 ml	apple juice
1–2 tbsp	pear purée, depending on the sweetness of the apples

Preparation

Wash and quarter the apples (peeling is not essential). Then cut the quarters in half again. Place in baking dish with lid, adding the spices and the juice, cover and bake at 170 °C for 30–35 minutes. Remove orange and lemon peel after cooking. Serve lukewarm.

The dish is more festive if you add half-whipped, vanilla-flavoured cream, or vanilla ice cream. You can also add dried apricots to the apples, and then less pear purée is needed as sweetener.

Sweet dumplings

Preparation time	2 hours including baking	
Ingredients	15 g	fresh yeast
	200 ml	milk
	15 g	sugar
	350 g	semi-white flour (strong bread flour)
	40 g	butter
	1	egg
	3 g	salt
	20 g	butter for baking
	20 g	sugar for baking
	200 ml	milk

Preparation   Starter dough: Dissolve the yeast in the lukewarm milk (200 ml) and place in a mixing bowl with the sugar and 100 g flour. Stir well, cover and leave to rise in a warm place.

Now add the rest of the flour, and the butter, egg, and salt, and knead until you get a soft, smooth dough. Leave to rise again for 20 minutes. Knead the dough together, and weigh out portions of approx. 70 g each. Form these into balls and place in a greased baking tray. The distance between each ball should be about 3 cm. Cover, and leave to rise, until the balls have almost doubled in size. Slightly warm the other batch of milk, and dissolve the sugar and butter in this. Add to the balls, cover and bake at 200 °C for about 25 minutes. Take off lid and put back in oven for a further 5 minutes, increasing the temperature to 220 °C. The dumplings are perfect when lightly browned on top, and with a caramelized crust below. Serve with dried fruit compote (see recipe p. 246).

The dough is very good for baking Easter hares.

Vanilla cream

Preparation time   20 minutes

Ingredients
500 ml   milk
50 g   cane sugar
½   vanilla pod
1 pinch   salt
20 g   cornflour
3   egg yolks
100 ml   cream

Preparation   Halve the vanilla pod lengthways and bring to the boil with 400 ml of the milk, the sugar and the salt. Stir the cornflour and the egg yolk with the rest of the milk until smooth, and then stir into the boiling fluid. Bring back to the boil while stirring, remove from heat and pass through sieve. Leave to cool, stirring occasionally. Whip the cream until stiff and fold into the dessert. Serve with a fruit garnish.

For vanilla pudding: Add 50 g butter to the still-hot mixture and then pour into pudding dishes rinsed in cold water. Turn out and serve garnished with whipped cream and fruits.

Sweet puddings and desserts

Vanilla sauce

Preparation time

Preparation   20 minutes
time

Ingredients   250 ml   milk
               ½   vanilla pod, cut open lengthways
               1 pinch   salt
               50 g   cane sugar
               1   egg yolk
               50 ml   milk
               10 g   cornflour
               50 ml   cream

Preparation   Bring to the boil the 250 ml milk with the vanilla pod, the sugar and the salt. Stir the cornflour and egg yolk with the rest of the milk until smooth, and then stir into the boiling fluid. Bring back to the boil while stirring, pass through a sieve, then leave to cool, stirring occasionally. The best way is to place it inside a bowl of water. After cooling, fold in the cream. You can also half whip the cream before folding in, which gives the sauce greater volume and a more satiny consistency.

Wheat and nut cream

A classic dessert

Preparation time	30 minutes	
Ingredients	60 g	wheat, freshly milled
	40 g	dates, chopped
	300 ml	water
	1 pinch	coriander seeds, milled
	60 g	hazelnuts, finely grated
	½ tsp	lemon peel, finely grated
	150 ml	cream
		fruit to garnish

Preparation	Stir the wheat with the dates into the cold water, add a pinch of salt and bring to the boil while stirring. Simmer for 10 minutes, then cover and leave to cool. Add the hazelnuts and the lemon peel, and stir vigorously with the whisk. Whip the cream and fold into the dessert. Serve garnished with fruit.

Lemon balm
Melissa officinalis

Lemon balm is warm and a man who eats thereof will laugh gladly, for its warmth affects the spleen and thus the heart is made to rejoice. But he in whose eye the white grows, let him pull the plant from the earth with its root, and let him place the uprooted plant straight away overnight in the water of a bubbling spring, and then let him warm the plant in a bowl after it has been brought forth again from the spring. And thus warmed let him lay it upon the eye during three nights, and the white in his eye will be healed and vanish.

Hildegard of Bingen

Bedouin muesli

An Arab version

Preparation time	30 minutes

Ingredients

1	orange
½	lemon
75 g	figs
125 g	dates
25 g	wheat, coarsely ground
250 ml	water
100 g	quark (curd cheese)
1 tbsp (20 g)	almond paste
250 g	apples

Preparation

Press the orange and the lemon. Cut the figs and dates into small pieces and soak in the pressed juice. Boil up the wheat meal and water together for 5 minutes, then leave to cool. Add the soaked fruit, the quark and almond paste to the porridge mix, and blend. Grate the apples and fold in. Serve garnished with fruit pieces.

Muesli

Bircher muesli

The original muesli (1 portion)

Preparation time	10 minutes

Ingredients		
	1 tbsp (20 g)	fine oatflakes
	3 tbsp	water
	½	lemon, the juice
	1 tbsp	hazelnuts, roasted and grated
	1 tbsp	cream or yoghurt
	200 g	apples
	1 tsp	pear purée

Preparation	Soak the oatflakes for 10 minutes in water, then add the lemon juice, hazelnuts and cream. Remove the bloom from the apples and grate them into the oatflakes using a Bircher grater.* Blend well immediately so that the apple stays white. Sweeten with honey or pear purée. The muesli can also be prepared using other fruit, primarily berries.
	If you use coarse oatflakes these will need to be soaked in water for several hours. The muesli should be prepared directly before it is eaten.

---

* This can be ordered from Switzerland via the internet. The Swiss name is 'Bircherraffel'.

Budwig muesli

Preparation time	10 minutes	
Ingredients	100 g	quark (curd cheese)
	1 tbsp	linseed oil, cold pressed
	3 tbsp (50 ml)	milk, preferably unpasteurized
	1 tbsp	honey
	150 g	fruit: apples, berries, bananas, etc.
Preparation	Stir together the quark with the linseed oil, milk and honey until smooth. Add the chopped fruit and blend together well.	

Muesli

Kollath muesli

Preparation time	30 minutes	
Ingredients	50 g	figs
	50 g	dates
	25 g	raisins
	160 g	wheat, freshly milled (coarse)
		water for soaking
	2	bananas
	250 g	apples
	50 ml	cream
		lemon juice
		honey as desired
	1 tbsp	hazelnuts

Preparation   Roughly chop the figs and dates and place in bowl with the raisins and the wheat meal. Add water so that it just covers the wheat, cover and place in fridge overnight. Next morning mash the bananas, grate the apples using the Bircher grater* and add to the soaked mix with the cream. Blend well and serve sprinkled with roasted, coarsely crushed hazelnuts.

---

* This can be ordered from Switzerland via the internet. The Swiss name is 'Bircherraffel'.

Clove
Syzygium aromaticum

The clove is very warm and has also a certain moisture within it, by means of which it expands pleasantly, similar to the pleasant moisture of honey. And if someone should have a headache so that his head does hum as though he were deaf, let him often eat of cloves and that will diminish the humming in his head. And if sick innards in man do sometimes swell, then it will often happen that such swelling of the innards causes dropsy in him. If this dropsy does begin to grow in him, let him often eat of cloves, and these will suppress the sickness for their strength passes into his innards and diminishes their swelling, and thus puts dropsy to flight so that it cannot increase further. But also if the warmth of the marrow in man repeatedly sweats, this will be the cause of foot gout in him. If this sickness begins to grow in a man, let him eat of cloves often and their strength will enter the marrow and prevent the increase of the foot gout, and the spread of it further through him, if it be still at its beginning. And he who is plagued by hiccups, let him eat often of cloves. But let him also take to him zedoary (white turmeric) after eating, and let him do this for the space of a month.

Hildegard of Bingen

Barley water

Refreshing grain drink

Preparation time	10 minutes + cooking time + soaking time

Ingredients		
	100 g	barley
	2 l	water
	2	figs
	1 tsp	ginger, cut into slices
	½	lemon, the peel
		lemon juice
	1 l	apple juice
	1 pinch	salt
		pear purée as desired

Preparation	Soak the barley with the figs in the water for 6–8 hours, add the ginger and simmer for one hour. Now add the lemon peel, cover and leave to absorb for 2–3 hours. Strain and blend the fluid with the apple juice. Flavour with lemon juice, pear purée and a pinch of salt. Is tasty either hot or cold. Without juice and spices this drink is highly recommended for stomach and intestinal disorders.

Drinks

Elderflower syrup

Very refreshing

Preparation time	approx. 2 hours

Ingredients

1.5 l	water
1.5 kg	cane sugar
400 g	elderflowers, freshly picked
200 ml	lemon juice, freshly pressed

Preparation   Select good quality blossoms and place in a pot with well-sealed lid. Bring to the boil the water and the sugar and pour hot on the blossoms. Cover well and leave for 24 hours. Strain through a cloth, add the lemon juice and bring to the boil. Fill bottles while boiling hot, and seal. Will keep for at least a year. To drink, dilute 1 part cordial with 8 to 10 parts water. Tastes good both hot and cold.

Herb tea

Preparation time	10–20 minutes

Ingredients		
	1l	water
	4–6 tsp	tea herbs

Preparation

Bring the water to the boil and before it is fully bubbling pour over the tea herbs. Cover and allow to draw for 3–10 minutes, then remove the herbs.

The length of infusing depends on the type of tea.

Blossom teas such as camomile are ready after 3 minutes. Leaves need about 4–5 minutes, and seeds such as caraway or fennel need to draw for up to 10 minutes.